STUDY GUIDE for

S0-BUA-709

DISCOVERING COMPUTERS

A Link to the Future

WORLD WIDE WEB ENHANCED

Gary B. Shelly
Thomas J. Cashman
William J. Dorin

Contributing Author
Tim. J. Walker

SHELLY
CASHMAN
SERIES®

COURSE TECHNOLOGY

COURSE TECHNOLOGY
ONE MAIN STREET
CAMBRIDGE MA 02142

an International Thomson Publishing company I(T)P·

CAMBRIDGE • ALBANY • BONN • CINCINNATI • LONDON • MADRID • MELBOURNE

MEXICO CITY • NEW YORK • PARIS • SAN FRANCISCO • TOKYO • TORONTO • WASHINGTON

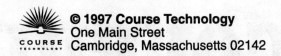
© 1997 Course Technology
One Main Street
Cambridge, Massachusetts 02142

I(T)P® International Thomson Publishing
The ITP logo is a registered trademark
of International Thomson Publishing.

Printed in the United States of America
For more information, contact Course Technology:

Course Technology
One Main Street
Cambridge, Massachusetts 02142, USA

International Thomson Publishing Europe
Berkshire House
168-173 High Holborn
London, WC1V 7AA, United Kingdom

Thomas Nelson Australia
102 Dodds Street
South Melbourne
Victoria 3205 Australia

Nelson Canada
1120 Birchmont Road
Scarborough, Ontario
Canada, M1K 5G4

International Thomson Editores
Campos Eliseos 385, Piso 7
Colonia Polanco
11560 Mexico D.F. Mexico

International Thomson Publishing GmbH
Konigswinterer Strasse 418
53227 Bonn, Germany

International Thomson Publishing Asia
Block 211, Henderson Road #08-03
Henderson Industrial Park
Singapore 0315

International Thomson Publishing Japan
Hirakawa-cho Kyowa Building, 3F
2-2-1 Hirakawa-cho, Chiyoda-ku
Tokyo 102, Japan

ISBN 0-7895-2849-5

3 4 5 6 7 8 9 10 BC 1 0 9 8

STUDY GUIDE FOR
DISCOVERING COMPUTERS
A LINK TO THE FUTURE
WORLD WIDE WEB ENHANCED

CONTENTS

PREFACE vi

TO THE STUDENT 1.2

- **CHAPTER ONE**
  AN OVERVIEW OF USING COMPUTERS
  Chapter Overview **1.5**
  Chapter Objectives **1.5**
  Chapter Outline **1.5**
  Terms **1.9**
  Self Test **1.10**
      True/False **1.10**
      Matching **1.10**
      Multiple Choice **1.11**
      Fill in the Blanks **1.12**
      Complete the Table **1.13**
      Things to Think About **1.13**
      Puzzle **1.14**
  Self Test Answers **1.15**

- **CHAPTER TWO**
  SOFTWARE APPLICATIONS:
  USER TOOLS
  Chapter Overview **2.1**
  Chapter Objectives **2.1**
  Chapter Outline **2.1**
  Terms **2.8**
  Self Test **2.9**
      True/False **2.9**
      Matching **2.9**
      Multiple Choice **2.10**
      Fill in the Blanks **2.11**
      Complete the Table **2.12**

Things to Think About **2.12**
Puzzle **2.13**
Self Test Answers **2.14**

- **CHAPTER THREE**
  THE SYSTEM UNIT
  Chapter Overview **3.1**
  Chapter Objectives **3.1**
  Chapter Outline **3.1**
  Terms **3.7**
  Self Test **3.8**
      True/False **3.8**
      Matching **3.8**
      Multiple Choice **3.9**
      Fill in the Blanks **3.10**
      Complete the Table **3.11**
      Things to Think About **3.11**
      Puzzle **3.12**
  Self Test Answers **3.13**

- **CHAPTER FOUR**
  INPUT AND OUTPUT
  Chapter Overview **4.1**
  Chapter Objectives **4.1**
  Chapter Outline **4.1**
  Terms **4.9**
  Self Test **4.11**
      True/False **4.11**
      Matching **4.11**
      Multiple Choice **4.12**
      Fill in the Blanks **4.13**
      Complete the Table **4.14**
      Things to Think About **4.15**

Puzzle **4.15**
Self Test Answers **4.17**

♦ **CHAPTER FIVE**
DATA STORAGE
Chapter Overview **5.1**
Chapter Objectives **5.1**
Chapter Outline **5.1**
Terms **5.6**
Self Test **5.6**
    True/False **5.6**
    Matching **5.7**
    Multiple Choice **5.8**
    Fill in the Blanks **5.9**
    Complete the Table **5.10**
    Things to Think About **5.10**
    Puzzle **5.11**
Self Test Answers **5.12**

♦ **CHAPTER SIX**
COMMUNICATIONS AND NETWORKS
Chapter Overview **6.1**
Chapter Objectives **6.1**
Chapter Outline **6.1**
Terms **6.9**
Self Test **6.10**
    True/False **6.10**
    Matching **6.10**
    Multiple Choice **6.12**
    Fill in the Blanks **6.12**
    Complete the Table **6.13**
    Things to Think About **6.13**
    Puzzle **6.14**
Self Test Answers **6.15**

♦ **CHAPTER SEVEN**
THE INTERNET AND ONLINE SERVICES
Chapter Overview **7.1**
Chapter Objectives **7.1**
Chapter Outline **7.1**
Terms **7.7**
Self Test **7.8**
    True/False **7.8**
    Matching **7.8**
    Multiple Choice **7.9**
    Fill in the Blanks **7.10**
    Complete the Table **7.11**
    Things to Think About **7.11**
    Puzzle **7.12**
Self Test Answers **7.13**

♦ **CHAPTER EIGHT**
OPERATING SYSTEMS AND SYSTEM SOFTWARE
Chapter Overview **8.1**
Chapter Objectives **8.1**
Chapter Outline **8.1**
Terms **8.7**
Self Test **8.8**
    True/False **8.8**
    Matching **8.8**
    Multiple Choice **8.9**
    Fill in the Blanks **8.10**
    Complete the Table **8.11**
    Things to Think About **8.11**
    Puzzle **8.11**
Self Test Answers **8.13**

♦ **CHAPTER NINE**
DATA MANAGEMENT AND DATABASES
Chapter Overview **9.1**
Chapter Objectives **9.1**
Chapter Outline **9.1**
Terms **9.6**
Self Test **9.7**
    True/False **9.7**
    Matching **9.7**
    Multiple Choice **9.8**
    Fill in the Blanks **9.9**
    Complete the Table **9.10**
    Things to Think About **9.10**
    Puzzle **9.10**
Self Test Answers **9.12**

♦ **CHAPTER TEN**
INFORMATION SYSTEMS
Chapter Overview **10.1**
Chapter Objectives **10.1**
Chapter Outline **10.1**
Terms **10.6**
Self Test **10.6**
    True/False **10.6**
    Matching **10.7**
    Multiple Choice **10.7**
    Fill in the Blanks **10.9**
    Complete the Table **10.10**
    Things to Think About **10.10**
    Puzzle **10.11**
Self Test Answers **10.12**

◆ **CHAPTER ELEVEN**
INFORMATION SYSTEMS DEVELOPMENT
Chapter Overview **11.1**
Chapter Objectives **11.1**
Chapter Outline **11.1**
Terms **11.9**
Self Test **11.10**
    True/False **11.10**
    Matching **11.10**
    Multiple Choice **11.11**
    Fill in the Blanks **11.12**
    Complete the Table **11.13**
    Things to Think About **11.13**
    Puzzle **11.14**
Self Test Answers **11.15**

◆ **CHAPTER TWELVE**
PROGRAM DEVELOPMENT AND
PROGRAMMING LANGUAGES
Chapter Overview **12.1**
Chapter Objectives **12.1**
Chapter Outline **12.1**
Terms **12.10**
Self Test **12.11**
    True/False **12.11**
    Matching **12.11**
    Multiple Choice **12.12**
    Fill in the Blanks **12.13**
    Complete the Table **12.14**
    Things to Think About **12.14**
    Puzzle **12.15**
Self Test Answers **12.16**

◆ **CHAPTER THIRTEEN**
SECURITY, PRIVACY, AND ETHICS
Chapter Overview **13.1**
Chapter Objectives **13.1**
Chapter Outline **13.1**
Terms **13.7**
Self Test **13.8**
    True/False **13.8**
    Matching **13.8**
    Multiple Choice **13.9**
    Fill in the Blanks **13.10**
    Complete the Table **13.11**
    Things to Think About **13.12**
    Puzzle **13.12**
Self Test Answers **13.14**

◆ **CHAPTER FOURTEEN**
MULTIMEDIA
Chapter Overview **14.1**
Chapter Objectives **14.1**
Chapter Outline **14.1**
Terms **14.7**
Self Test **14.8**
    True/False **14.8**
    Matching **14.9**
    Multiple Choice **14.9**
    Fill in the Blanks **14.10**
    Complete the Table **14.11**
    Things to Think About **14.12**
    Puzzle **14.12**
Self Test Answers **14.13**

PREFACE

This Study Guide is intended as a supplement to *Discovering Computers: A Link to the Future, World Wide Web Enhanced*. A variety of activities are provided in a format that is easy to follow and facilitates learning the material presented by helping students recall, review, and master introductory computer concepts. Each chapter in the Study Guide includes:

- A Chapter Overview summarizing the chapter's content that helps students recall the general character of the topics presented.

- Chapter Objectives specifying the goals students should have achieved after finishing the chapter.

- A partial Chapter Outline designed to be completed by the students, helping them to identify, organize, and recognize the relationships among important concepts.

- A list of Terms defined in the chapter, along with the pages where they are found.

- A Self Test, together with answers, that assists students in addressing their mastery of the subject matter through true/false, matching, multiple choice, fill in the blanks, and complete the table questions.

- Questions suggesting Things to Think About, calculated to help students develop a deeper understanding of the information in the chapter.

- A Puzzle that supplies a more entertaining approach to reviewing important terms and concepts.

In addition to the activities in each chapter, the Study Guide also offers a To the Student section that provides tips on effectively using the textbook, attending class, preparing for and taking tests, and utilizing the Study Guide.

Acknowledgments

The Shelly Cashman Series would not be the most successful computer textbook series ever published without the contributions of outstanding publishing professionals. First, and foremost, among them is Becky Herrington, director of production and designer. She is the heart and soul of the Shelly Cashman Series, and it is only through her leadership, dedication, and untiring efforts that superior products are produced.

Under Becky's direction, the following individuals made significant contributions to this book: Peter Schiller, production manager; Ginny Harvey, series specialist and developmental editor; Ken Russo, Mike Bodnar, and Greg Herrington, graphic artists; Stephanie Nance, graphic artist and cover designer; Jeanne Black, interior design; Patti Koosed, editorial assistant; Nancy Lamm, proofreader; Sarah Evertson of Image Quest, photo researcher; and Cristina Haley, indexer.

Special thanks go to Jim Quasney, our dedicated series editor; Lisa Strite, senior product manager; Lora Wade, associate product manager; Scott MacDonald, editorial assistant; and Sarah McLean, marketing director.

Our sincere thanks go to Dennis Tani, who together with Becky Herrington, designed *Discovering Computers: A Link to the Future, World Wide Web Enhanced* and performed all the layout and typography, executed the magnificent drawings contained in the book, and survived an impossible schedule with goodwill and amazing patience. We are in awe of Dennis's incredible work.

We hope you find using this Study Guide an enriching and rewarding experience.

Gary B. Shelly
Thomas J. Cashman
William J. Dorin

Shelly Cashman Series – Traditionally Bound Textbooks

The Shelly Cashman Series presents computer textbooks across the entire spectrum including both Windows- and DOS-based personal computer applications in a variety of traditionally bound textbooks, as shown in the table below. For more information, see your Course Technology representative or call 1-800-648-7450.

COMPUTERS	
Computers	Discovering Computers: A Link to the Future, World Wide Web Enhanced
	Discovering Computers: A Link to the Future, World Wide Web Enhanced Brief Edition
	Using Computers: A Gateway to Information, World Wide Web Edition
	Using Computers: A Gateway to Information, World Wide Web Brief Edition
	Exploring Computers: A Record of Discovery 2e with CD-ROM
	A Record of Discovery for Exploring Computers 2e
	Study Guide for Discovering Computers: A Link to the Future, World Wide Web Enhanced
	Study Guide for Using Computers: A Gateway to Information, World Wide Web Edition
	Brief Introduction to Computers (32-page)
WINDOWS APPLICATIONS	
Integrated Packages	Microsoft Office 97: Introductory Concepts and Techniques
	Microsoft Office 97: Advanced Concepts and Techniques
	Microsoft Office 95: Introductory Concepts and Techniques
	Microsoft Office 95: Advanced Concepts and Techniques
	Microsoft Office 4.3 running under Windows 95: Introductory Concepts and Techniques
	Microsoft Office for Windows 3.1 Introductory Concepts and Techniques Enhanced Edition
	Microsoft Office: Introductory Concepts and Techniques
	Microsoft Office: Advanced Concepts and Techniques
	Microsoft Works 4* • Microsoft Works 3.0* • Microsoft Works 2.0 — Short Course
Windows	Introduction to Microsoft Windows NT Workstation 4
	Microsoft Windows 95: Introductory Concepts and Techniques (96-page)
	Introduction to Microsoft Windows 95 (224-page)
	Microsoft Windows 95: Complete Concepts and Techniques
	Microsoft Windows 3.1 Introductory Concepts and Techniques
	Microsoft Windows 3.1 Complete Concepts and Techniques
Word Processing	Microsoft Word 97* • Microsoft Word 7* • Microsoft Word 6* • Microsoft Word 2.0
	Corel WordPerfect 7 • WordPerfect 6.1* • WordPerfect 6* • WordPerfect 5.2
Spreadsheets	Microsoft Excel 97* • Microsoft Excel 7* • Microsoft Excel 5* • Microsoft Excel 4
	Lotus 1-2-3 97* • Lotus 1-2-3 Release 5* • Lotus 1-2-3 Release 4* • Quattro Pro 6 • Quattro Pro 5
Database Management	Microsoft Access 97* • Microsoft Access 7* • Microsoft Access 2
	Paradox 5 • Paradox 4.5 • Paradox 1.0 • Visual dBASE 5/5.5
Presentation Graphics	Microsoft PowerPoint 97* • Microsoft PowerPoint 7* • Microsoft PowerPoint 4*
Personal Information Management	Microsoft Outlook 97 Mail (with Mail simulator)
DOS APPLICATIONS	
Operating Systems	DOS 6 Introductory Concepts and Techniques
	DOS 6 and Microsoft Windows 3.1 Introductory Concepts and Techniques
Integrated Package	Microsoft Works 3.0
Word Processing	WordPerfect 6.1 • WordPerfect 6.0
	WordPerfect 5.1 Step-by-Step Function Key Edition • WordPerfect 5.1 Function Key Edition
Spreadsheets	Lotus 1-2-3 Release 4 • Lotus 1-2-3 Release 2.4 • Lotus 1-2-3 Release 2.3
	Lotus 1-2-3 Release 2.2 • Lotus 1-2-3 Release 2.01
	Quattro Pro 3.0 • Quattro with 1-2-3 Menus (with Educational Software)
Database Management	dBASE 5 • dBASE IV Version 1.1 • dBASE III PLUS (with Educational Software)
	Paradox 4.5 • Paradox 3.5 (with Educational Software)
PROGRAMMING AND NETWORKING	
Programming	Microsoft Visual Basic 4 for Windows 95* (available with Student version software)
	Microsoft Visual Basic 3.0 for Windows*
	QBasic • QBasic: An Introduction to Programming • Microsoft BASIC
	Structured COBOL Programming (Micro Focus COBOL also available)
Networking	Novell NetWare for Users
	Business Data Communications: Introductory Concepts and Techniques
Internet	The Internet: Introductory Concepts and Techniques (UNIX)
	Netscape Navigator 4: An Introduction
	Netscape Navigator 3: An Introduction • Netscape Navigator 2 running under Windows 3.1
	Netscape Navigator: An Introduction (Version 1.1)
	Netscape Composer
	Microsoft Internet Explorer 3: An Introduction
SYSTEMS ANALYSIS	
Systems Analysis	Systems Analysis and Design, Second Edition

*Also available as a Double Diamond Edition, which is a shortened version of the complete book

Shelly Cashman Series – **Custom Edition**® Program

If you do not find a Shelly Cashman Series traditionally bound textbook to fit your needs, the Shelly Cashman Series unique **Custom Edition** program allows you to choose from a number of options and create a textbook perfectly suited to your course. Features of the **Custom Edition** program are:

- Textbooks that match the content of your course

- Windows- and DOS-based materials for the latest versions of personal computer applications software

- Shelly Cashman Series quality, with the same full-color materials and Shelly Cashman Series pedagogy found in the traditionally bound books

- Affordable pricing so your students receive the **Custom Edition** at a cost similar to that of traditionally bound books

The table on the right summarizes the available materials. For more information, see your Course Technology representative or call 1-800-648-7450.

For Shelly Cashman Series information, visit Shelly Cashman Online at **www.scseries.com**

COMPUTERS	
Computers	Discovering Computers: A Link to the Future, World Wide Web Enhanced
	Discovering Computers: A Link to the Future, World Wide Web Enhanced Brief Edition
	Using Computers: A Gateway to Information, World Wide Web Edition
	Using Computers: A Gateway to Information, World Wide Web Brief Edition
	A Record of Discovery for Exploring Computers 2e (available with CD-ROM)
	Study Guide for Discovering Computers: A Link to the Future, World Wide Web Enhanced
	Study Guide for Using Computers: A Gateway to Information, World Wide Web Edition
	Introduction to Computers (32-page)

OPERATING SYSTEMS	
Windows	Microsoft Windows 95: Introductory Concepts and Techniques (96-page)
	Introduction to Microsoft Windows NT Workstation 4
	Introduction to Microsoft Windows 95 (224-page)
	Microsoft Windows 95: Complete Concepts and Techniques
	Microsoft Windows 3.1 Introductory Concepts and Techniques
	Microsoft Windows 3.1 Complete Concepts and Techniques
DOS	Introduction to DOS 6 (using DOS prompt)
	Introduction to DOS 5.0 or earlier (using DOS prompt)

WINDOWS APPLICATIONS	
Integrated Packages	Microsoft Works 4*
	Microsoft Works 3.0* • Microsoft Works 3.0 — Short Course
Microsoft Office	Using Microsoft Office 97 (16-page)
	Using Microsoft Office (16-page)
	Object Linking and Embedding (OLE) (32-page)
	Microsoft Outlook 97
	Microsoft Outlook 97 Mail (with Mail simulator)
	Microsoft Schedule+ 7
	Introduction to Integrating Office 95 Applications (80-page)
Word Processing	Microsoft Word 97* • Microsoft Word 7* • Microsoft Word 6* • Microsoft Word 2.0
	Corel WordPerfect 7 • WordPerfect 6.1* • WordPerfect 6* • WordPerfect 5.:
Spreadsheets	Microsoft Excel 97* • Microsoft Excel 7* • Microsoft Excel 5* • Microsoft Excel 4
	Lotus 1-2-3 97* • Lotus 1-2-3 Release 5* • Lotus 1-2-3 Release 4*
	Quattro Pro 6 • Quattro Pro 5
Database Management	Microsoft Access 97* • Microsoft Access 7* • Microsoft Access 2*
	Paradox 5 • Paradox 4.5 • Paradox 1.0 • Visual dBASE 5/5.5
Presentation Graphics	Microsoft PowerPoint 97* • Microsoft PowerPoint 7* • Microsoft PowerPoint 4*

DOS APPLICATIONS	
Integrated Package	Microsoft Works 3.0
Word Processing	WordPerfect 6.1 • WordPerfect 6.0
	WordPerfect 5.1 Step-by-Step Function Key Edition
	WordPerfect 5.1 Function Key Edition
	Microsoft Word 5.0
Spreadsheets	Lotus 1-2-3 Release 4 • Lotus 1-2-3 Release 2.4 • Lotus 1-2-3 Release 2.3
	Lotus 1-2-3 Release 2.2 • Lotus 1-2-3 Release 2.01
	Quattro Pro 3.0 • Quattro with 1-2-3 Menus
Database Management	dBASE 5 • dBASE IV Version 1.1 • dBASE III PLUS
	Paradox 4.5 • Paradox 3.5

PROGRAMMING AND NETWORKING	
Programming	Microsoft Visual Basic 4 for Windows 95* (available with Student version software) • Microsoft Visual Basic 3.0 for Windows*
	Microsoft BASIC • QBasic
Networking	Novell NetWare for Users
Internet	The Internet: Introductory Concepts and Techniques (UNIX)
	Netscape Navigator 4: An Introduction
	Netscape Navigator 3: An Introduction
	Netscape Navigator 2 running under Windows 3.1
	Netscape Navigator: An Introduction (Version 1.1)
	Netscape Composer
	Microsoft Internet Explorer 3: An Introduction

*Also available as a mini-module

STUDY GUIDE FOR
DISCOVERING COMPUTERS
A LINK TO THE FUTURE
WORLD WIDE WEB ENHANCED

TO THE STUDENT 1.2

♦ **CHAPTER ONE**
AN OVERVIEW OF USING COMPUTERS
Chapter Outline 1.5
Self Test 1.10
Self Test Answers 1.15

♦ **CHAPTER TWO**
SOFTWARE APPLICATIONS:
USER TOOLS
Chapter Outline 2.1
Self Test 2.9
Self Test Answers 2.14

♦ **CHAPTER THREE**
THE SYSTEM UNIT
Chapter Outline 3.1
Self Test 3.8
Self Test Answers 3.13

♦ **CHAPTER FOUR**
INPUT AND OUTPUT
Chapter Outline 4.1
Self Test 4.11
Self Test Answers 4.17

♦ **CHAPTER FIVE**
DATA STORAGE
Chapter Outline 5.1
Self Test 5.6
Self Test Answers 5.12

♦ **CHAPTER SIX**
COMMUNICATIONS AND NETWORKS
Chapter Outline 6.1
Self Test 6.10
Self Test Answers 6.15

♦ **CHAPTER SEVEN**
THE INTERNET AND ONLINE SERVICES
Chapter Outline 7.1
Self Test 7.8
Self Test Answers 7.13

♦ **CHAPTER EIGHT**
OPERATING SYSTEMS AND SYSTEM SOFTWARE
Chapter Outline 8.1
Self Test 8.8
Self Test Answers 8.13

♦ **CHAPTER NINE**
DATA MANAGEMENT AND DATABASES
Chapter Outline 9.1
Self Test 9.7
Self Test Answers 9.12

♦ **CHAPTER TEN**
INFORMATION SYSTEMS
Chapter Outline 10.1
Self Test 10.6
Self Test Answers 10.12

♦ **CHAPTER ELEVEN**
INFORMATION SYSTEMS DEVELOPMENT
Chapter Outline 11.1
Self Test 11.10
Self Test Answers 11.15

♦ **CHAPTER TWELVE**
PROGRAM DEVELOPMENT AND
PROGRAMMING LANGUAGES
Chapter Outline 12.1
Self Test 12.11
Self Test Answers 12.16

♦ **CHAPTER THIRTEEN**
SECURITY, PRIVACY, AND ETHICS
Chapter Outline 13.1
Self Test 13.8
Self Test Answers 13.14

♦ **CHAPTER FOURTEEN**
MULTIMEDIA
Chapter Outline 14.1
Self Test 14.8
Self Test Answers 14.13

TO THE STUDENT

Would you like to be promised success in this course? Your textbook, *Discovering Computers: A Link to the Future, World Wide Web Enhanced*, can be a source of the knowledge you will need to excel. Unfortunately, no textbook alone can guarantee mastery of the subject matter; genuine understanding depends largely on how hard you are willing to work. Other available resources, however, can *help* you get the most out of this course. That is the intent of this Study Guide.

Following are tips on using the textbook, attending class, preparing for and taking tests, and utilizing the Study Guide. Most of the tips in the first three areas not only will help to improve your performance in this course, they also can be applied to many of your other college classes. The tips in the last area are designed to explain how this Study Guide can enrich your understanding of the material in *Discovering Computers: A Link to the Future, World Wide Web Enhanced*.

Using the Textbook

The textbook is one of your most important tools in building a solid foundation in the subject matter. To use your textbook most effectively, follow these guidelines:

Survey the whole text first. The preface explains the authors' goals, objectives, point of view, assumptions, and pedagogical approach. The table of contents supplies an overview of the topics covered. See how chapters are organized, the way terms and concepts are indicated, how illustrations and tables are used, and the types of exercises that conclude each chapter. Look for special features interspersed throughout the book, and use the index to clarify information.

Start by skimming the chapter. Read the chapter introduction, which gives you a general idea of the chapter's content, and study the chapter objectives, which identify what you are expected to learn. Next, skim the chapter. Look at the section headings to get a feeling for how sections are related to each other. Notice bold or italic text; usually, these words are important. Finally, read the brief summary at the end of the chapter, which restates, in broad terms, the major concepts and conclusions offered in the chapter.

Carefully read the entire chapter. Some instructors prefer that you only skim a chapter before class, and then do a detailed reading after their lecture. Other instructors want you to read the chapter thoroughly before class. Whenever you sit down to read the entire chapter, first review the exercises at the end of the chapter to provide a more specific focus for your reading. As you read the text, make sure you understand all the terms and concepts. Pay particular attention to illustrations (photographs, diagrams, and tables) and their captions; often, they help clarify ideas in the text. Write in your book, highlight important points, note relationships, and jot questions. Read the Computers at Work and In the Future sections that conclude each chapter in *Discovering Computers: A Link to the Future, World Wide Web Enhanced* and determine how these sections are related to the subject of the chapter. Carefully examine the summary material (review) and list of terms (terms). If you do not remember or understand, go back and re-read the relevant sections. Do the exercises that deal specifically with the content of the chapter (yourTurn). Finally, complete any assigned additional exercises (hotTopics, outThere, winLabs, and webWalk).

Attending Class

Attending class is an essential ingredient to success in a course. Simply showing up, however, is not enough. To get the most out of class, follow these guidelines:

Arrive early and prepared. Sit close to the front of the room to hear well and see visual materials, such as transparencies, clearly. Have any necessary supplies, such as a notebook, writing implement, and your textbook. Be ready to start when your instructor begins.

Take notes. Note taking is essential to recall later the material presented in class. Note-taking styles vary: some people jot down key words and concepts, while others write narratives that are more detailed. The important thing is that the style you adopt works for you. If, when you later consult your notes, you find they do little to help you remember the subject of the lecture, try to be more comprehensive. If you find that in taking notes you frequently fall behind your instructor, try to be briefer. Review your notes as soon as possible after class, while the material is still fresh.

Do not be afraid to ask questions. Often, people hesitate to ask questions because they fear they will appear foolish. In reality, asking good questions is a sign of intelligence; after all, you have to be insightful enough to realize something is unclear. Keep in mind that often your classmates have the same questions you do. Good questions not only help clarify difficult topics, they also increase the depth of your understanding by suggesting relationships between ideas or establishing the impact of concepts. Learn the best time to ask questions. In small classes, sometimes it is possible to ask questions during a lecture. In a larger setting, it may be best to approach your instructor after class or make an appointment. If you feel really lost, your instructor may be able to recommend a peer tutor or an academic counseling service to help you.

Preparing for and Taking Tests

Tests are an opportunity for you to demonstrate how much you have learned. Many strategies are certain to improve performance on tests. To do your best on a test, follow these guidelines:

Find out as much as you can about the test. Ask your instructor what material will be covered, what types of questions will be used, how much time you will have, and what supplies you will need (pencil or pen, paper or bluebook, perhaps even notes or a textbook if it is an open-book test). You will be more likely to do your best work if there are no surprises. Occasionally, copies of previous tests are available from the department or school library. These are invaluable aids in test preparation.

Use your resources wisely. Start studying by reviewing your notes and, in *Discovering Computers: A Link to the Future, World Wide Web Enhanced*, the review section at the end of each chapter. Review carefully and attempt to anticipate some of the questions that may be asked. Re-read the sections in your textbook on topics you are not sure of or that seem especially important. Try to really comprehend, and not merely memorize, the material. If you truly understand a concept, you should be able to answer any question, no matter the type. Understanding often makes remembering easier, too; for example, if you know how a page printer works, it is simple to recall that page printer speed is measured in pages per minute (ppm). When memorizing is necessary, use whatever technique works (such as memory tricks, verbal repetition, flash cards, and so on).

Avoid cramming. To prepare for an athletic contest, you would not practice for twelve straight hours before the event. In the same way, you should not expect to do well on a test by spending the entire night before it cramming. When you cram, facts become easily confused, and anything you do keep them straight probably will be remembered only for a short time. It also is difficult to recognize how concepts are related, which can be an important factor in successful test taking. Try to study in increments over a period of time. Use the night before the test to do a general review of the pertinent material, concentrating on what seems most difficult. Then, get a good night's sleep so you are well rested and at your best when it is time for the test.

Take time to look through the test. Arrive early enough at the test site to settle in properly. Listen for any special instructions that might be given. Skim the entire test before you start. Read the directions carefully; not every question in each section may need answering, or you may be asked to answer questions in a certain way. Determine the worth of each part, the parts you think can be done most quickly, and the parts you believe will take the longest to complete. Use your assessment to budget your time.

Answer the questions you are sure of first. As you work through the test, read each question carefully and answer the easier ones first. If you are not certain of an answer, skip that question for now, ensuring you get the maximum number of "sure" points and allowing less worry about time when later dealing with the more difficult questions. Occasionally, you will find that the information you needed to answer one of the questions you skipped can be found elsewhere in the test. Other times, you suddenly will remember what you need to answer a question you skipped as you are dealing with another part of the test.

Use common sense. Most questions have logical answers. While these answers often require specific knowledge of the subject matter, sometimes it is possible to determine a correct answer with a general knowledge of the subject matter and a little common sense. As you work through a test, and when you go back over the test after you are finished, make sure all your answers are reasonable. Do not change an answer, however, unless you are sure your first answer was wrong. If incorrect answers are not penalized any more than having no answer at all, it is better to try a logical guess than to leave an answer blank. But, if you are penalized for incorrect answers (for example, if your final score is the number of correct answers minus the number of incorrect answers), you will have to decide whether or not to answer a question you are not sure of based on how confident you are of your guess.

Utilizing this Study Guide

The purpose of this Study Guide is to further your understanding of the concepts presented in *Discovering Computers: A Link to the Future, World Wide Web Enhanced*. The Study Guide chapter should be completed *after* you have finished the corresponding chapter in the book. The Study Guide chapters are divided into sections, each of which has a specific purpose:

Chapter Overview. This is a brief summary of the chapter's content that helps you recall the general character of the information dealt with in the chapter.

Chapter Objectives. This is a roster of the same objectives as the chapter in the book. After completing the chapter, review the Chapter Objectives to determine how many of them you have met. If you have not reached an objective, go back and review the appropriate material or your notes.

Chapter Outline. This is a partially completed outline of the chapter with page numbers where topics can be found. The Chapter Outline is designed to help you review the material and to assist you in organizing and seeing the relationships between concepts. Complete the outline in as much depth as you feel necessary. You can refer directly to the text as you work through the outline while re-reading the chapter, or you can fill in the outline on your own and then use the text to check your information.

Terms. This is a list of important terms to remember. Read the Terms and make sure you know them all. If necessary, go to the page number to familiarize yourself with a term's meaning.

Self Test. This is a tool you can use to evaluate your mastery of the chapter. The Self Test consists of five types of questions: true/false, matching, multiple choice, fill in the blanks, and complete the table. Take the test without referring to your textbook or notes. Leave any answer you are unsure of blank or, if you prefer, guess at the answer, but indicate you were unsure by placing a question mark (?) after your response. When you have finished the Self Test, check your work against the answers at the end of the Study Guide chapter. Each answer gives the page number in the text where the answer can be found. Review any solution that was incorrect or any reply that was uncertain.

Things to Think About. These questions help you better grasp the information in each chapter. Because specific answers to the Things to Think About questions will vary, no solutions are given. The true purpose of these questions is to get you to contemplate the 'why"behind concepts, thus encouraging you to gain a greater understanding of the concepts, their connections, and their significance.

Puzzle. This activity is designed to review important terms in an entertaining fashion. The Puzzle in each chapter is one of four types: a word search puzzle, a crossword puzzle, a puzzle involving words written in code, or a puzzle in which words must be placed in a grid. Every puzzle offers a definition or description and asks you to supply the associated term. The solution to each puzzle is given.

C H A P T E R   1
An Overview of Using Computers

CHAPTER OVERVIEW

This chapter presents a broad introduction to concepts and terminology that are related to computers. You learn the difference between computer literacy and information literacy. What a computer is, why a computer is so powerful, and how a computer knows what to do are explained. The information processing cycle is defined, the components of a computer are presented, and the five major categories of computers are described. You are introduced to computer software, discover the elements of an information system, and learn the meaning of connectivity. Finally, you are taken on a tour of a mid-sized company to find out how a typical business might use computers.

CHAPTER OBJECTIVES

After completing this chapter, you will be able to:

• Explain the difference between computer literacy and information literacy

• Define the term computer

• Identify the major components of a computer

• Explain the four operations of the information processing cycle: input, process, output, and storage

• Explain how speed, reliability, accuracy, storage, and communications make computers powerful tools

• Identify the categories of computers

• Explain the difference between system software and application software

• Describe how the six elements of an information system work together

CHAPTER OUTLINE

I. Computer and information literacy [p. 1.2]

Computer literacy is knowing how to use a computer.

Information literacy is _____

(continued)

II. What is a computer? [p. 1.4]

A computer is _____

_____

III. What are the components of a computer? [p. 1.4]

Data is input, processed, output, and stored by specific equipment called computer hardware.

A. Input devices [p. 1.4]

Used to _____

Two common input devices are the _____ and the _____

B. _____ [p. 1.6]

Is a box-like case that contains the electronic circuits that actually cause the processing of data to occur

Includes the central processing unit, memory, and other electronic components

The central processing unit (CPU) contains a control unit that _____

_____ and an arithmetic/logic (ALU) unit that _____

Memory, also called RAM (Random Access Memory) and main memory, stores _____

_____

C. Output devices [p. 1.6]

Convert results into a form that can be understood by the user

Three commonly used output devices are a _____, _____, and

_____

D. _____ [p. 1.7]

Store instructions and data when they are not being used by the system unit

A floppy disk is _____

Hard disk drives contain non-removable disks and provide larger storage capacities than floppy disks.

A CD-ROM drive _____

E. Communications devices [p. 1.7]

Enable a computer to connect to other computers

A modem is _____

A network interface card _____

_____ is called a network.

F. Peripheral devices [p. 1.7]

A peripheral device _____

IV. What does a computer do? [p. 1.7]

Computers perform the four general operations of the information processing cycle: _____,

_____, _____, and _____

Data refers to the raw facts, including numbers, words, images, and sounds, given to a computer during the input operation.

Information refers to _____

Information processing is the production of information by processing data on a computer.

Computer users (end users or users) are _____

_____

V. Why is a computer so powerful? [p. 1.8]

   A. Speed [p. 1.8]

      Data flows along a computer's circuits at close to the speed of light.

   B. _____ [p. 1.8]

      The electronic components in modern computers seldom fail.

   C. _____ [p. 1.8]

      Most instances of computer error can be traced back to other causes, often human mistakes

   D. Storage [p. 1.8]

      Computers can _____

   E. Communications [p. 1.8]

      If a computer is able to communicate _____

      _____

      Communications capability _____

VI. Connectivity [p. 1.9]

   • Connectivity refers to the ability to connect a computer to other computers.

   • Most business computers _____

   The global network of computers _____

   _____

   The World Wide Web (WWW) _____

   _____

VII. Categories of computers [p. 1.10]

   Computers generally are classified according to their _____, _____,

   _____, and _____

   A. Personal computers [p. 1.10]

      Is a small system designed to _____

      Classifications include: _____, _____,

      _____, _____, _____,

      _____, _____, _____,

      _____, and _____

   B. _____ [p. 1.13]

      Designed to support a computer network that allows users to share files, application software, and hardware

      Characteristics: _____

      _____

      _____

   C. Minicomputers [p. 1.14]

      More powerful than personal computers and can support a number of users performing different tasks

   D. Mainframe computers [p. 1.14]

(continued)

Large systems that can _____

_____

Usually require a specialized environment

E.   _____ [p. 1.15]

The most powerful and most expensive category of computers

Used for such applications as _____

VIII. Computer software [p. 1.16]

A computer program is a series of instructions that direct a computer.

Computer programmers _____

Programmers often follow a plan developed by a systems analyst who

_____

_____

A. System software [p. 1.17]

System software consists of_____

_____

Instructions in the operating system tell the computer _____

_____

B. User interface [p. 1.17]

The user interface _____

A graphical user interface (GUI) _____

_____

C. Application software [p. 1.18]

Programs required for common business and personal applications can be obtained from software vendors.

Purchased programs are _____

Some of the more widely used are _____, _____,

_____, _____, _____,

_____, and _____

IX. What are the elements of an information system? [p. 1.19]

Elements of an information system are _____, _____,

_____, _____, _____, and

_____

X. An example of how one company uses computers [p. 1.20]

A. Reception [p. 1.20]

Uses a computer to _____

B. Sales [p. 1.21]

Uses a computer to _____

C. Marketing [p. 1.21]

Uses a computer to _____

D. Shipping and receiving [p. 1.22]

Uses a computer to _____

E. Manufacturing [p. 1.22]

Uses a computer to _____

F. Product design [p. 1.23]

Uses a computer to _____

G. Accounting [p. 1.23]

Uses a computer to _____

H. Human resources [p. 1.24]

Uses a computer to _____

I. Information systems [p. 1.24]

Uses a computer to _____

J. Executive [p. 1.25]

Uses a computer to _____

K. Summary of how one company uses computers [p. 1.25]

Employees in each department also could use the computer for _____

TERMS

application software [p. 1.18]
application software packages
   [p. 1.18]
arithmetic/logic unit (ALU)
   [p. 1.6]
auxiliary storage devices
   [p. 1.7]

CD-ROM drive [p. 1. 7]
central processing unit (CPU)
   [p. 1.6]
communications devices [p. 1.7]
computer [p. 1.4]
computer literacy [p. 1.2]
computer program [p. 1.16]
computer programmers
   [p. 1.16]
computer system [p. 1.4]
computer users [p. 1.7]
connectivity [p. 1.9]
control unit [p. 1.6]

data [p. 1.7]
desktop computers [p. 1.13]

end users [p. 1.7]

floppy disk [p. 1.7]
floppy disk drive [p. 1.7]

graphical user interface (GUI)
   [p. 1.17]

hand-held computers [p. 1.10]
hard disk drive [p. 1.7]
hardware [p. 1.4]
home page [p. 1.8]

icon [p. 1.17]
information [p. 1.7]
information literacy [p. 1.2]
information processing
   [p. 1.7]
information processing cycle
   [p. 1.7]
information system [p. 1.19]
input [p. 1.7]
input devices [p. 1.4]
Internet [p. 1.3, 1.9]

keyboard [p. 1.4]

laptop computers [p. 1.13]

main memory [p. 1.6]
mainframe computers [p. 1.14]
memory [p. 1.6]
micro [p. 1.10]
microcomputer [p. 1.10]
minicomputers [p. 1.14]
modem [p. 1.7]
monitor [p. 1.6]
motherboard [p. 1.6]
mouse [p. 1.4]

mouse pointer [p. 1.4]
multimedia format [p. 1.9]

network [p. 1.7]
network computers (NC)
   [p. 1.13]
network interface card [p. 1.7]
notebook computers [p. 1.11]

operating system [p. 1.17]
output [p. 1.6, 1.7]
output devices [p. 1.6]

palmtop computers [p. 1.10]
pen computers [p. 1.10]
peripheral device [p. 1.7]
personal communicator [p. 1.11]
personal computer (PC) [p. 1.10]
personal digital assistant (PDA)
   [p. 1.11]
pointer [p. 1.4]
printer [p. 1.6]
process [p. 1.7]
processor [p. 1.6]

RAM (Random Access Memory)
   [p. 1.6]

secondary storage [p. 1.7]
server [p. 1.13]
server computers [p. 1.13]
(continued)

software [p. 1.16]
software package [p. 1.18]
speakers [p. 1.6]
storage [p. 1.7]
storage devices [p. 1.7]
subnotebook computers
   [p. 1.13]

supercomputers [p. 1.15]
system board [p. 1.6]
system software [p. 1.17]
system unit [p. 1.6]
systems analyst [p. 1.16]
tower computers [p. 1.13]
user interface [p. 1.17]

users [p. 1.7]
Web browser programs [p. 1.9]
Web sites [p. 1.9]
workstations [p. 1.13]
World Wide Web (WWW)
   [p. 1.9]

SELF TEST
True/False

_____ 1. Information literacy is related to computers because, increasingly, information is available from sources that can be accessed using computers.

_____ 2. In the central processing unit (CPU), the control unit performs math and logic operations.

_____ 3. Secondary storage devices temporarily store data and program instructions when they are being processed.

_____ 4. Information processing is the production of information by processing data on a computer.

_____ 5. Most reports about computer errors usually are traced to the unreliability of the computer's electronic components.

_____ 6. Computers generally are classified according to their size, speed, processing capabilities, and price.

_____ 7. Server computers usually are designed to be connected to one or more networks and have the most powerful CPUs available.

_____ 8. Computer hardware is the key to productive use of computers.

_____ 9. Some of the more widely used application software packages are word processing, desktop publishing, electronic spreadsheet, presentation graphics, database, communications, and electronic mail.

_____ 10. Obtaining useful and timely information requires only computer equipment and software.

Matching

1. _____ computer literacy
2. _____ monitor
3. _____ data
4. _____ information
5. _____ laptop computers
6. _____ mainframe computers
7. _____ systems analyst
8. _____ system software
9. _____ graphical user interface (GUI)
10. _____ information system

a. programs related to controlling the actual operation of computer equipment

b. one of three commonly used output devices

c. writes the instructions necessary to direct the computer to process data into information

d. hardware, software, users, personnel, data, and procedures

e. knowing how to use a computer

f. together with the user and programmer, determines and designs desired program output

g. part of an operating environment that provides visual clues to help the user

h. knowing how to find, analyze, and use information

i. raw facts given to a computer during the input operation

j. consists of programs that tell a computer how to produce information

k. large systems that usually require a specialized environment

l. the most powerful and most expensive category of computers

m. comparisons of data to see if one value is greater than, equal to, or less than another

n. larger versions of notebook computers that weigh between eight and fifteen pounds

o. input that has been processed into a meaningful and useful form

Multiple Choice

_____ 1. Which of the following are examples of input devices?

    a. the keyboard and the mouse

    b. the central processing unit (CPU) and main memory

    c. the printer and the monitor

    d. floppy disks and hard disks

_____ 2. In the information processing cycle, what happens during the output operation?

    a. data is entered into the computer

    b. the computer manipulates data to create information

    c. the information created is put into some form that people can use

    d. the computer can communicate with other computers

_____ 3. What component of a computer system is _not_ considered a peripheral device?

    a. input devices

    b. the system unit

    c. output devices

    d. secondary storage devices

_____ 4. The computer's power is derived from which of these capabilities?

    a. speed

    b. reliability

    c. storage

    d. all of the above

_____ 5. Palmtop computers, notebook computers, and desktop computers are all examples of what category of computers?

    a. minicomputers

    b. servers

    c. personal computers

    d. mainframe computers

_____ 6. What are workstations?

    a. personal computers that are usually designed for a specific purpose and are used by workers who are on their feet instead of sitting at a desk

    b. smaller versions of notebook computers that generally weigh less than four pounds

    c. expensive, high-end personal computers with powerful calculating and graphics capabilities that are frequently used by engineers

    d. specialized portable personal computers that use a pen-like device to enter data

(continued)

_____ 7. What is the most powerful category of computers and, accordingly, the most expensive?
    a. personal computers
    b. supercomputers
    c. mainframe computers
    d. server computers

_____ 8. Who writes the detailed set of instructions necessary to direct a computer to process data into information?
    a. end users
    b. systems analysts
    c. computer programmers
    d. information technicians

_____ 9. What is application software?
    a. programs related to controlling the actual operations of computer equipment
    b. programs that must be stored in main memory for a computer to operate
    c. programs that work with the operating system to make the computer easier to use
    d. programs that tell a computer how to produce information

_____ 10. Which of the following elements of an information system documents computer operations and related operations, thus helping the entire system run efficiently?
    a. software
    b. procedures
    c. data
    d. users

Fill in the Blanks

1. _____ is defined as knowing how to find, analyze, and use information.

2. Data is processed by specific equipment that often is called computer _____.

3. The _____ of a computer contains the electronic circuits that actually cause the processing of data to occur.

4. The _____ contains a control unit and an arithmetic/logic unit (ALU).

5. The operations that comprise the _____ are: input, process, output, and storage.

6. _____ refers to the ability to connect a computer to other computers.

7. _____ are the most common type of personal computer and are designed to fit conveniently on the surface of a workspace.

8. _____ are more powerful than personal computers, can support a number of users performing different tasks, and can cost from approximately $15,000 to several hundred thousand dollars.

9. The instructions in the _____, an important part of system software, tell the computer how to perform functions such as load, store, and execute a program and transfer data among the system devices and memory.

10. Each _____ in a graphical user interface represents an application software package or a file or document where data is stored.

Complete the Table

Category	Physical Size	Speed (in MIPS)	Number of Online Users	General Price Range
Personal Computer	hand-held to desktop or tower	_____ _____	usually single user	_____ _____
Server	_____ _____	100 to 300 MIPS	_____ _____	$5,000 to $150,000
Minicomputer	small cabinet to several large cabinets	_____ _____	2 to 4,000 users	_____ _____
Mainframe	_____ _____	hundreds of MIPS	_____ _____	$300,000 to several million $
Supercomputer	full room of equipment	_____ _____	hundreds of users	_____ _____

Things to Think About

1. Do the four operations in the information processing cycle (input, process, output, storage) always have to be performed in order? Why or why not?

2. Why is each component of a computer system (input devices, system unit, output devices, secondary storage devices, communications devices) important?

3. It is easy to see why most of the elements of an information system are significant, but why are documented procedures important? In what way do they help the entire system run efficiently?

4. What role does connectivity play in increasing information literacy?

Puzzle

All of the words described below appear in the puzzle. Words may be either forward or backward, across, up and down, or diagonal. Circle each word as you find it.

```
M A I N M E M O R Y A U
O S S E C O R P F Q L S
U N ▢ E G A R O T S U E
S T N K S I D D R A H R
E O Z T N I G T I U P S
P W A T E U U N U D C U
O E E Y G G F L O P P Y
I R B U K R O W T E N C
N O I T A M R O F N I I
T M A I N F R A M E U ▢
E K E Y B O A R D A T A
R N O T E B O O K N G W
```

raw facts given to a computer during the input operation

small plastic disk that stores data as magnetic areas

data processed into a meaningful and useful form

information processing cycle operation in which data is entered

information processing cycle operation in which data is manipulated to create information

information processing cycle operation in which data is kept for future use

common input device on which data is typed

small symbol that appears on the computer screen, often in the shape of an arrow

abbreviation for part of CPU that performs math and logic operations

commonly used output device

type of storage devices that store data instructions and data when they are not being used

abbreviation for the small computer systems that have become widely used

personal computer small enough to be carried in a briefcase

type of personal computer in an upright case

powerful machines that can handle many users and process large volumes of data

formed when computers are connected together

the key to productive use of computers

stores data and programs when they are being processed

abbreviation for a user interface that uses icons

SELF TEST ANSWERS

True/False	Matching	Multiple Choice
1. *T* [p. 1.2]	1. *e* [p. 1.2]	1. *a* [p. 1.4]
2. *F* [p. 1.6]	2. *b* [p. 1.6]	2. *c* [p. 1.6]
3. *F* [p. 1.7]	3. *i* [p. 1.7]	3. *b* [p. 1.7]
4. *T* [p. 1.7]	4. *o* [p. 1.7]	4. *d* [p. 1.8]
5. *F* [p. 1.8]	5. *n* [p. 1.13]	5. *c* [p. 1.10]
6. *T* [p. 1.10]	6. *k* [p. 1.14]	6. *c* [p. 1.13]
7. *T* [p. 1.13]	7. *f* [p. 1.16]	7. *b* [p. 1.15]
8. *F* [p. 1.16]	8. *a* [p. 1.17]	8. *c* [p. 1.16]
9. *T* [p. 1.18]	9. *g* [p. 1.17]	9. *d* [p. 1.18]
10. *F* [p. 1.19]	10. *d* [p. 1.19]	10. *b* [p. 1.19]

Fill in the Blanks

1. *Information literacy* [p. 1.2]
2. *hardware* [p. 1.4]
3. *system unit* [p. 1.6]
4. *central processing unit (CPU)* [p. 1.6]
5. *information processing cycle* [p. 1.7]
6. *Connectivity* [p. 1.9]
7. *Desktop computers* [p. 1.13]
8. *Minicomputers* [p. 1.14]
9. *operating system* [p. 1.17]
10. *icon* [p. 1.17]

Complete the Table [p. 1.10]

Category	Physical Size	Speed (in MIPS)	Number of Online Users	General Price Range
Personal Computer	hand-held to desktop or tower	*1 to 200 MIPS*	usually single user	*hundreds to several thousand $*
Server	*tower or small cabinet*	100 to 300 MIPS	*2 to 1,000 users*	$5,000 to $150,000
Minicomputer	small cabinet to several large cabinets	*hundreds of MIPS*	2 to 4,000 users	*$15,000 to several hundred thousand $*
Mainframe	*partial to full room of equipment*	hundreds of MIPS	*hundreds to thousands of users*	$300,000 to several million $
Supercomputer	full room of equipment	*thousands of MIPS*	hundreds of users	*several million $ and up*

Puzzle Answer

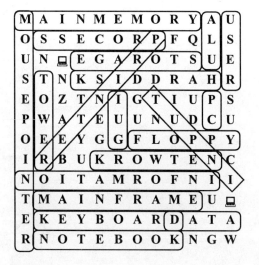

CHAPTER 2
Software Applications: User Tools

CHAPTER OVERVIEW

This chapter introduces fifteen widely used computer software applications, sometimes referred to as productivity software. The purpose of a user interface is explained, and you discover some of the characteristics of a graphical user interface. The general features of word processing, desktop publishing, spreadsheet, database, presentation graphics, communications, electronic mail, personal information management, and project management software are described. You learn about the variety of productivity tools offered by integrated software. Finally, some of the aids and support tools for application users are discussed.

CHAPTER OBJECTIVES

After completing this chapter, you will be able to:

• Define and describe a user interface and a graphical user interface

• Explain the key features of widely used software applications

• Explain the advantages of integrated software and software suites

• Explain object linking and embedding

• List and describe learning aids and support tools that help you to use personal computer software applications

CHAPTER OUTLINE

I. The operating system and user interface [p. 2.2]

Before any application software is run, the operating system must be loaded from the hard disk into the memory of the computer and started.

The operating system tells _____

The way the software communicates with you _____

A user interface is _____

_____

The graphical user interface, or GUI (pronounced gooey), combines _____

(continued)

Microsoft Windows (referred to as Windows) is the most popular graphical user interface for personal computers.

Common features of a GUI:

icons — _____

windows — _____

_____ — _____

_____ — _____

II. Software applications [p. 2.4]

The fifteen widely used personal computer software applications are: _____,

_____, _____, _____,

_____, _____, _____,

_____, _____, _____,

_____, _____, _____,

_____, and _____

A. Word processing software [p. 2.4]

Enables a computer to produce or modify documents that consist primarily of _____

Dedicated word processing systems, _____

Producing a document using word processing usually consists of four steps: creating, editing, formatting, and printing. A fifth step, saving the document, should be performed frequently.

1. Creating a word processing document [p. 2.4]

Involves entering the text, usually using the keyboard

Features used:

- Word wrap – automatic line return when text reaches a certain position

- Scrolling – _____

- _____ – _____
  _____

2. Editing a word processing document [p. 2.6]

Making changes in the content of a document

Features used:

- Insert and delete – _____

- Cut, copy, and paste – _____

- _____ – _____

- _____ – _____

- _____ – _____

- Thesaurus – _____

- _____ – _____

- _____ – _____

3. Formatting a word processing document [p. 2.8]

Changing the appearance of a document

Features used:

• Typeface, font, and style – _____

_____

• Margins and alignment – _____

_____

• _____ – _____

_____

• _____ – _____

• Columns and tables – _____

• _____ – _____

_____

• Borders and shading – _____

_____

• Page numbers, headers, and footers – _____

_____

• _____ – _____

4. Printing a word processing document [p. 2.11]

Available options:

• Number of copies and pages – _____

• Portrait and landscape – _____

_____

• _____ – _____

5. Creating Web pages using a word processor [p. 2.12]

Today, the major word processors support _____

_____

B.　Desktop publishing software [p. 2.12]

Allows you to design and produce high-quality documents that contain _____

_____

Page composition and layout, sometimes called page makeup, _____

_____

The text and graphics used by a DTP program are _____

Illustration software is used _____

Distinguishing features: _____

_____

_____

Relies on a page definition language, such as PostScript, that _____

_____

Popular DTP packages: _____

(continued)

C. _____ [p. 2.14]

Organizes numeric data into a format called a spreadsheet or worksheet

A spreadsheet file is like _____

Data is organized vertically in columns and horizontally in rows

A cell is _____

Cells may contain three types of data: labels (text), values (_____), and

_____ that perform calculations on the data in a spreadsheet.

Functions are _____

A macro is _____

Formulas copied to a new cell can be updated automatically (_____) or continue

to refer to the same cell location (_____).

A spreadsheet's capability to recalculate when data is changed makes it a valuable tool for decision making.

What-if analysis is a term that describes _____

_____

A standard feature is the ability to create charts that _____

_____

Analytical graphics or business graphics are _____

Three basic chart types: _____, _____, and

_____.

Popular spreadsheet packages: _____

D. Database software [p. 2.21]

A database refers to a collection of data that is stored in files.

Database software allows _____

_____

A file is _____

Each record contains _____

Type of data that could be in each field:

- _____ – _____
- _____ – _____
- _____ – _____
- _____ – _____
- _____ – _____

Validation is _____

A query is _____

Popular database packages: _____

E. Presentation graphics software [p. 2.24]

Allows the user to create documents, called slides, used in making presentations

Features included with most packages: _____

_____

Besides slides, can create _____, _____, and

_____

A slide sorter _____ _____

Popular presentation graphics packages: _____

F. Communications software and Web browsers [p. 2.26]

Communications software is used to transmit data from one computer to another.

For two computers to communicate, _____

_____

_____

_____

Communications software helps manage communications tasks by:

- _____
- _____
- _____
- _____

Frequently used by employees away from the office

1. Online services [p. 2.26]

   Communications software also is used to access online services for news, weather, financial, and travel information.

   Some online service companies are _____

   Popular communications software packages: _____

2. Web browsers [p. 2.26]

   A special type of _____

   _____

   Information at Internet Web sites _____

   The first page of a Web site _____

   Widely used browsers today: _____

G. Electronic mail software [p. 2.27]

   Also called e-mail, allows you to _____

   _____

   E-mail etiquette rules: _____

   _____

   _____

   Popular e-mail packages: _____

H. _____ [p. 2.28] .

   Helps you keep track of miscellaneous bits of personal information

(continued)

Capabilities offered: _____

_____

Popular PIM packages: _____

I. Personal finance software [p. 2.29]

Helps you to track _____

Financial planning features include _____

_____

_____

Popular personal financial applications packages: _____

J. Project management software [p. 2.29]

Allows you _____

_____

Popular project management packages: _____

K. _____ [p. 2.30]

Helps companies record and report their financial transactions

Additional tasks that accounting software handle:

• _____

• _____

• _____

• _____

• Payroll; amounts owed to employees

• _____

• _____

• _____

Popular small business accounting packages: _____

L. Groupware [p. 2.30]

Loosely defined term _____

_____

Part of a broad concept _____

_____

Features:

• _____ – _____

• Group Scheduling – _____

• _____ – _____

• _____ – _____

Popular groupware packages: _____

M. Computer-aided design (CAD) software [p. 2.31]

Assists you _____

CAD programs are used in such applications as _____, _____,

_____ , and _____

Popular CAD packages: _____

N.   Multimedia authoring software [p. 2.32]

Allows you _____

_____

A multimedia presentation _____

_____

Multimedia ToolBook by Asymetrix Corporation is a widely-used multimedia authoring package.

O.   Integrated software and software suites [p. 2.32]

Refers to packages that _____

_____

These applications have consistent command and menu structures and the capability to transfer data between applications.

Sometimes criticized as being _____

Popular integrated software packages: _____

Software suites are _____

Advantages of software suites: _____

_____

Popular software suites: _____

III. Object linking and embedding (OLE) [p. 2.34]

Referred to by acronym _____

_____

An object can be _____

A source document _____

The destination document _____

A compound document _____

1. Both object linking and object embedding allow _____

2. With an embedded object, _____

_____

3. With a linked object, _____

_____

4. With linked objects the change process works both ways.

IV. Learning aids and support tools for application users [p. 2.36]

Available learning aids and support tools:

_____ – refers to explanatory information that is available while you are using an

application

Tutorials —step-by-step instructions that show how to use an application

_____ – _____

_____ – _____

TERMS

absolute referencing [p. 2.19]
accounting software [p. 2.30]
alignment [p. 2.9]
alphanumeric [p. 2.22]
analytical graphics [p. 2.20]
annotations [p. 2.8]
AutoCorrect [p. 2.7]
AutoFormat [p. 2.10]
AutoSave [p. 2.4]
AutoSum button [p. 2.16]

bar charts [p. 2.20]
border [p. 2.10]
built-in style [p. 2.10]
business graphics [p. 2.20]
button [p. 2.3]

cell [p. 2.15]
centered alignment [p. 2.9]
chart [p. 2.20]
clip art [p. 2.10]
Clipboard [p. 2.6]
color libraries [p. 2.13]
columns [p. 2.13, 2.15]
commands [p. 2.3]
communications software
    [p. 2.26]
compound document [p. 2.34]
computer-aided design (CAD)
    [p. 2.31]
context-sensitive [p. 2.36]
copy [p. 2.6]
currency [p. 2.22]
cursor [p. 2.6]
cut [p. 2.6]

database [p. 2.21]
database software [p. 2.21]
date [p. 2.22]
dedicated word processing
    systems [p. 2.4]
delete [p. 2.6]
desktop publishing (DTP)
    [p. 2.12]
destination document [p. 2.34]

editing [p. 2.6]
electronic mail software [p. 2.27]
e-mail [p. 2.27]
embedded object [p. 2.34]

fields [p. 2.21]
file [p. 2.21]
font [p. 2.9]
footers [p. 2.10]
format [p. 2.8]

formulas [p. 2.15]
functions [p. 2.16]

grammar checker [p. 2.8]
graphical user interface (GUI)
    [p. 2.2]
graphics [p. 2.10]
groupware [p. 2.30]

headers [p. 2.10]
highlighting tool [p. 2.8]
home page [p. 2.26]

icons [p. 2.2]
illustration software [p. 2.13]
insert [p. 2.6]
insertion point [p. 2.6]
integrated software [p. 2.32]

justification [p. 2.9]
justified alignment [p. 2.9]

labels [p. 2.15]
landscape [p. 2.11]
left alignment [p. 2.9]
line charts [p. 2.20]
line spacing [p. 2.9]
linked object [p. 2.35]

macro [p. 2.16]
margins [p. 2.9]
memo [p. 2.22]
menu [p. 2.3]
Microsoft Windows [p. 2.2]
monospacing [p. 2.9]
multimedia authoring software
    [p. 2.32]
multimedia presentation [p. 2.32]

numeric [p. 2.22]

object [p. 2.34]
object linking and embedding
    [p. 2.34]
OLE [p. 2.34]
online Help [p. 2.36]
operating system [p. 2.2]

page composition and layout
    [p. 2.12]
page definition language
    [p. 2.14]
page makeup [p. 2.12]
Paste [p. 2.6]
personal finance software
    [p. 2.29]
personal information management
    (PIM) software [p. 2.28]

pie charts [p. 2.20]
point [p. 2.8]
portrait [p. 2.11]
PostScript [p. 2.14]
presentation graphics [p. 2.24]
print preview [p. 2.11]
project management software
    [p. 2.29]
proportional spacing [p. 2.9]

query [p. 2.23]

record [p. 2.21]
relative referencing [p. 2.19]
replace [p. 2.6]
revision marks [p. 2.8]
right alignment [p. 2.9]
rows [p. 2.15]

scroll tips [p. 2.6]
scrolling [p. 2.6]
search [p. 2.6]
shading [p. 2.10]
slides [p. 2.24]
software packages [p. 2.4]
software suite [p. 2.33]
source document [p. 2.34]
spacing [p. 2.9]
spelling checker [p. 2.6]
spreadsheet [p. 2.14]
style [p. 2.9]
style sheet [p. 2.10]

tables [p. 2.10]
template [p. 2.10]
thesaurus [p. 2.8]
trade books [p. 2.37]
tutorials [p. 2.36]
typeface [p. 2.8]

user interface [p. 2.2]

validation [p. 2.23]
values [p. 2.15]

Web browser [p. 2.26]
Web pages [p. 2.26]
what-if analysis [p. 2.19]
window [p. 2.2]
wizard [p. 2.36]
word processing [p. 2.4]
word wrap [p. 2.5]
workgroup technology [p. 2.30]
worksheet [p. 2.14]
WYSIWYG [p. 2.5]

SELF TEST
True/False

_____ 1. One of the more common user interfaces is the graphical user interface (GUI), which combines text and graphics to make software easier to use.

_____ 2. The fifteen widely used personal computer software applications are used by a small number of organizations and individuals, usually for entertainment.

_____ 3. Portrait printing means the paper is wider than it is tall.

_____ 4. A page definition language describes the DTP document to be printed in a language the printer can understand.

_____ 5. In a spreadsheet, labels help identify the data and help organize the worksheet.

_____ 6. Each field in a database contains a collection of related facts called records.

_____ 7. Presentation graphics software allows you to efficiently create professional quality presentations that help communicate information more effectively.

_____ 8. For two computers to communicate, they need only be connected by some type of link, such as a telephone line.

_____ 9. Project management software helps you keep track of the miscellaneous bits of personal information that each of us deals with every day.

_____ 10. With a linked object, changes made in the source document are automatically made in the destination document.

Matching

1. _____   WordPerfect, Microsoft Word

2. _____   QuarkXPress, PageMaker

3. _____   Lotus 1-2-3, Microsoft Excel, Corel Quattro Pro

4. _____   Microsoft Access, dBASE, FoxPro, Paradox

5. _____   Aldus Persuasion, Microsoft PowerPoint, Lotus Freelance Graphics, Compel

6. _____   Crosstalk, Procomm Plus

7. _____   Netscape Navigator, Microsoft Internet Explorer

8. _____   Microsoft Mail, Lotus cc:Mail, Eudora

9. _____   Timeline, Microsoft Project

10. _____   Microsoft Works, ClarisWorks

a. popular communications software packages

b. popular database packages

c. popular integrated software packages

d. popular word processing packages

e. popular presentation graphics packages

f. popular e-mail packages

g. popular keyboard templates

h. popular software suites

i. popular tutorial packages

j. popular desktop publishing packages

k. popular Web browsers

l. popular online Help packages

m. popular trade books

n. popular spreadsheet packages

o. popular project management packages

Multiple Choice

_____ 1. In a graphical user interface, what is a menu?
  a. a rectangular area of the screen used to present information
  b. a picture or symbol used to represent processing options
  c. a list of options from which the user can choose
  d. an icon that causes a specific action to take place

_____ 2. Which of the following is _not_ one of the fifteen most widely used personal computer software applications?
  a. point-of-sale (POS)
  b. electronic mail (e-mail)
  c. desktop publishing (DTP)
  d. personal information management (PIM)

_____ 3. In word processing, what is WYSIWYG?
  a. the capability to increase or decrease the size of graphics objects
  b. the capability to rotate text and graphics objects
  c. the capability to easily add or delete entire columns or pages
  d. the capability to display information on the screen exactly as it will look when printed

_____ 4. When creating a document using word processing, what happens during the formatting step?
  a. text is entered, usually by using the keyboard
  b. changes are made to the content of the document
  c. the appearance of a document is changed
  d. all of the above

_____ 5. In an electronic spreadsheet, what are numbers in a cell called?
  a. labels
  b. values
  c. formulas
  d. functions

_____ 6. Which of the following would be considered alphanumeric information in a database field?
  a. XYZ555 (a license plate number)
  b. $7.25 (an hourly wage)
  c. 25,463 (the number of items on hand)
  d. 06/11/97 (a date)

_____ 7. Which of the following is _not_ a feature included with most presentation graphics packages?
  a. numerous chart types
  b. what-if analysis
  c. special effects
  d. image libraries

_____ 8. Which of the following is _not_ a common sense rule of e-mail etiquette?
  a. never use abbreviations, even if they are understood easily
  b. avoid using e-mail for trivia, gossip, or other non-essential communications
  c. keep the distribution list to a minimum
  d. read your mail regularly and clear messages that are no longer needed

_____ 9. Outliners are one of the capabilities of personal information management software. For what purpose are outliners used?
  a. to schedule activities for a particular day and time

b. to rough out an idea by constructing and reorganizing a framework of important points and subpoints

c. to record comments and assign them to one or more categories that can be used to retrieve the comments

d. to search files for specific words and phrases

_____ 10. What are wizards?

a. step-by-step instructions using real examples that show how to use an application

b. additional instructions available within the application

c. books available to help in learning to use the features of application packages

d. automated assistants that help you complete a task

Fill in the Blanks

1. In a graphical user interface (GUI), _____ are instructions that cause the computer software to perform specific actions.

2. A software product within a category is called a(n) _____.

3. A(n) _____ allows you to look up synonyms for words in a document while you are using your word processor.

4. In DTP, collections of _____ contain several hundred to several thousand images grouped by type.

5. A(n) _____ in a spreadsheet cell performs calculations on the data and displays the resulting value in the cell.

6. A(n) _____ refers to a collection of data that is stored in files.

7. Presentation graphics software allows the user to create documents, called _____, that are used in making presentations before a group.

8. To make the sending of messages efficient, _____ software allows the user to send a single message to a distribution list consisting of two or more individuals.

9. The value of _____ software is that it provides a method for managers to control and manage the variables of an undertaking to help ensure the undertaking will be completed on time and within budget.

10. _____, such as Microsoft Office and Lotus SmartSuite, are individual applications packaged in the same box and sold for a price significantly less than buying the applications individually.

Complete the Table

SPREADSHEET FUNCTIONS	
FINANCIAL	
FV (rate, number of periods, payment)	Calculates the future value of an investment.
NPV (rate, range)	
_____	Calculates the periodic payment for an annuity.
DAY & TIME	
NOW	_____
MATHEMATICAL	
_____	Rounds a number down to the nearest integer.
ROUND (number, number of digits)	
_____	Calculates the square root of a number.
SUM (range)	
STATISTICAL	
	Calculates the average value of a range of numbers.
STDEV (range)	_____
LOGICAL	
_____	Performs a test and returns one value if the test is true and another value if the test is false.

Things to Think About

1. Why is WYSIWYG an important capability of desktop publishing software?
2. Why is a spreadsheet's capability to perform what-if analysis important to business executives?
3. What types of software would be particularly useful to business travelers? Why?
4. Why are word processing and spreadsheet packages the most widely used productivity software in business? Why are personal information management and project management packages used less frequently?

Puzzle

Across

1. type of (2) down software that allows you to organize numeric data in a worksheet or table format
5. business or analytical pictures created by spreadsheets; also used as clip art and for presentation software
9. remove text from a document
10. name a popular data communications software package
11. type of chart used to show the relationship of data
12. feature that finds all occurrences of a particular character, word, or combination of words
14. automatic line return when text reaches a certain point
16. abbreviation for type of software that allows you to design and produce professional looking documents
19. add text to a document
21. collection of related data organized in records
22. remove a portion of a document and store it electronically

Down

2. general category name for the fifteen most widely used personal computer software packages
3. specific set of characters that are designed the same
4. type of chart effective for showing the relationship of parts to a whole
6. contains a collection of related facts
7. symbol that indicates where on the screen the next character will appear
8. list of options from which the user can choose
13. the same information found at the top of each page
15. measure of typeface size, approximately 1/72 of an inch
17. abbreviation for type of software that helps you keep track of personal information
18. the intersection where a column and row meet
20. horizontal organization of data in a spreadsheet

SELF TEST ANSWERS

True/False

1. *T* [p. 2.2]
2. *F* [p. 2.4]
3. *F* [p. 2.11]
4. *T* [p. 2.14]
5. *T* [p. 2.15]
6. *F* [p. 2.21]
7. *T* [p. 2.25]
8. *F* [p. 2.26]
9. *F* [p. 2.29]
10. *T* [p. 2.35]

Matching

1. *d* [p. 2.12]
2. *j* [p. 2.14]
3. *n* [p. 2.20]
4. *b* [p. 2.23]
5. *e* [p. 2.25]
6. *a* [p. 2.26]
7. *k* [p. 2.26]
8. *f* [p. 2.28]
9. *o* [p. 2.29]
10. *c* [p. 2.33]

Multiple Choice

1. *c* [p. 2.3]
2. *a* [p. 2.4]
3. *d* [p. 2.4]
4. *c* [p. 2.8]
5. *b* [p. 2.15]
6. *a* [p. 2.22]
7. *b* [p. 2.24]
8. *a* [p. 2.28]
9. *b* [p. 2.28]
10. *d* [p. 2.36]

Fill in the Blanks

1. *commands* [p. 2.3]
2. *software package* [p. 2.4]
3. *thesaurus* [p. 2.8]
4. *clip art* [p. 2.10]
5. *formula* [p. 2.15]
6. *database* [p. 2.21]
7. *slides* [p. 2.24]
8. *electronic mail (e-mail)* [p. 2.27]
9. *project management* [p. 2.29]
10. *Software suites* [p. 2.33]

Complete the Table [p. 2.16]

SPREADSHEET FUNCTIONS	
FINANCIAL	
FV (rate, number of periods, payment)	Calculates the future value of an investment.
NPV (rate, range)	*Calculates the net present value of an investment.*
PMT (rate, number of periods, present value)	Calculates the periodic payment for an annuity.
DAY & TIME	
NOW	*Returns the current date and time.*
MATHEMATICAL	
INT (number)	Rounds a number down to the nearest integer.
ROUND (number, number of digits)	*Rounds a number to a specified number of digits.*
SQRT (number)	Calculates the square root of a number.
SUM (range)	*Calculates the total of a range of numbers.*
STATISTICAL	
AVERAGE (range)	Calculates the average value of a range of numbers.
STDEV (range)	*Calculates the standard deviation of a range of numbers.*
LOGICAL	
IF (logical test, value if true, value if false)	Performs a test and returns one value if the test is true and another value if the test is false.

Puzzle Answer

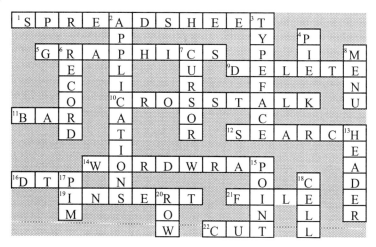

C H A P T E R   3
The System Unit

CHAPTER OVERVIEW

This chapter examines the components of the system unit, describes how memory stores programs and data, and discusses the sequence of operations that occurs when instructions are executed on a computer. You discover what the system unit is and how data is represented electronically. You learn how the binary number system is used to represent data. The components of the system unit are described, including the motherboard, microprocessor and CPU, upgrade sockets, memory, coprocessors, buses, expansion slots, ports and connectors, bays, power supply, and sound components. Machine language instructions are explained and various types of processing are detailed. Finally, you learn how a computer chip is manufactured.

CHAPTER OBJECTIVES

After completing this chapter, you will be able to:

- Define a bit and describe how a series of bits in a byte is used to represent data
- Discuss how bit pattern codes are used to represent characters
- Identify the components of the system unit and describe their use
- Describe how the CPU uses the four steps of the machine cycle to process data
- Describe the primary use and characteristics of RAM and ROM memory
- Explain the difference between parallel and serial ports
- Describe a machine language instruction and the instruction set of a computer
- Describe various types of processing including pipelining, parallel processing, and neural networks
- Explain how computers use the binary number system
- Explain how a computer chip is made

CHAPTER OUTLINE

I. What is the system unit? [p. 3.2]

It is in the system unit that _____

The system unit contains _____

(continued)

II. How data is represented in a computer [p. 3.3]

Most computers are digital computers, meaning _____

_____

Converting data into a digital form is called digitizing.

Analog computers are designed to _____

In a computer, only two digits are used _____

_____

A bit is _____

A byte is _____

  A. ASCII and EBCDIC [p. 3.4]

    The American Standard Code for Information Interchange, called ASCII, is _____

    _____

    The Extended Binary Coded Decimal Interchange Code or EBCDIC, is _____

    _____

  B. Unicode [p. 3.4]

    Asian and other languages use a different alphabet.

    Many of these languages _____

    Unicode is a 16-bit code that has the capacity _____

    Unicode is currently implemented _____

  C. Parity [p. 3.5]

    A parity bit is _____

    In computers with odd parity, _____

    In computers with even parity, _____

III. The components of the system unit [p. 3.6]

Usually are contained in a metal or plastic case; for PCs, all components usually are in a single box

IV. Motherboard [p. 3.7]

The motherboard sometimes called the main board or system board, is _____

_____

V. Microprocessor and the CPU [p. 3.7]

The microprocessor is a single integrated circuit on a personal computer that contains the CPU (central processing unit).

An integrated circuit (chip or IC) is _____

The central processing unit (CPU) contains _____

  A. The control unit [p. 3.8]

    Can be thought of as the *brain* of the computer.

    Operates by repeating the four operations of the machine cycle: _____,

    _____, _____, and _____.

    Fetching means _____

    Decoding is _____

Executing refers _____

Storing takes place _____

B. The arithmetic/logic unit [p. 3.8]

The arithmetic/logic unit (ALU) contains the electronic circuitry necessary to _____

Arithmetic operations include _____

Logical operations consist of _____

C. Registers [p. 3.8]

Registers, contained in both the control unit and the ALU, are _____

_____

D. The system clock [p. 3.8]

Used by the control unit to _____

Generates electronic pulses at a fixed rate measured in megahertz (MHz).

E. Word size [p. 3.9]

Word size is _____

The larger the word size of the CPU, the faster the capability of the computer to process data.

F. Microprocessor comparison [p. 3.10]

PC microprocessors most often are identified by their model number or model name.

VI. Upgrade sockets [p. 3.10]

Some motherboards contain upgrade sockets that can be used to _____

_____

VII. Memory [p. 3.11]

Refers to integrated circuits that temporarily store program instructions and data that can be retrieved

Memory chips are installed on the motherboard and also on similar circuit boards that control computer devices such as printers.

A. RAM [p. 3.11]

RAM (random access memory) is _____

RAM memory is said to be volatile because _____

_____

Flash RAM (flash memory) is _____

Today, most RAM memory is installed by using a SIMM (single in-line memory module) or _____

Cache memory is _____

Level 1 (L1) or internal cache is built into the microprocessor chip itself.

Level 2 (L2) cache is usually _____

B. ROM [p. 3.13]

ROM (read only memory) is _____

ROM memory is described as nonvolatile because _____

_____

Firmware or microcode are instructions stored in main memory.

(continued)

   C.   CMOS [p. 3.13]

       CMOS (complementary metal-oxide semiconductor) memory is used _____

       The system information in the CMOS _____

_____

       Unlike ROM memory, _____

   D.   Memory speed [p. 3.13]

       Access speed is _____

       Measured in nanoseconds (one billionth of a second)

       Most memory is comprised of _____

       RAM cache memory is comprised of _____

       Static RAM chips are _____

_____

       Registers and level 1 cache designed into the CPU chip are the fastest type of memory.

       One millisecond is a thousandth of a second.

VIII. Coprocessors [p. 3.14]

     A coprocessor is _____

   A.   Buses [p. 3.14]

       A bus is _____

       An expansion bus carries _____

       A local bus is _____

       Buses can transfer multiples of eight bits at a time; the larger the number of bits handled, the faster the computer can transfer data.

  IX.   Expansion slots [p. 3.15]

     An expansion slot is _____

     The circuit board for the add-on device is called an expansion board (expansion card, controller card, adapter card, or interface card).

     PC Cards are used for _____

   X.   Ports and connectors [p. 3.16]

     A port is _____

     Ports have different types of connectors, that are used to attach cables to peripheral devices.

   A.   Parallel ports [p. 3.16]

       Parallel ports transfer _____

       A SCSI port can be used to _____

   B.   Serial ports [p. 3.18]

       A serial port transmits _____

       A MIDI port is designed to _____

       Newer technology, such as the Universal Serial Bus (USB), _____

  XI.   Bays [p. 3.18]

     A bay (or drive bay) is _____

     Rails are mounting brackets that are sometimes required to install a device in a bay.

A cage is two or more bays side by side or on top of one another.

External bays, which have one end adjacent to an opening in the case, are used for _____

_____

Internal bays, which are not accessible from outside the case, are used for _____

XII. Power supply [p. 3.18]

The power supply converts _____

XIII. Sound components [p. 3.18]

Most PCs have the capability to generate sounds through a small speaker housed within the system unit

By installing expansion boards, _____

XIV. Summary of the components of the system unit [p. 3.19]

Information presented about the various components of the system unit

The next section will _____

_____

XV. Machine language instructions [p. 3.19]

A machine language instruction is _____

_____

The instruction set contains _____

CISC (*complex instruction set computing or computers*) have hundreds of commands in their instruction sets.

RISC (*reduced instruction set computing or computers*) technology increases overall processing capability by

_____

An operation code, the first part of a machine language instruction, tells _____

_____

An operand, the second part of a machine language instruction, specifies _____

_____

Today, program instructions are written in readable form using a variety of programming languages.

Computer speed can be rated by the number of machine language instructions processed in one second.

One MIPS equals _____

The term megaflops (MFLOPS) is used for _____

Gigaflops (GFLOPS) is used for _____

XVI. Types of processing [p. 3.21]

   A. Pipelining [p. 3.21]

   In most CPUs, the system unit waits until an instruction completes all four stages of the machine cycle before beginning to work on the next instruction.

   With pipelining, a new instruction is fetched _____

   Superscaler CPUs _____

   B. Parallel processing [p. 3.21]

   Another way to speed processing is to use more than one CPU in a computer.

   Parallel processing involves _____

(continued)

Massively parallel processors (MPPs) use _____

C. Neural network computers [p. 3.22]

Use _____

XVII. Number systems [p. 3.22]

The binary number system is used to represent the electronic status of the bits in memory.

Hexadecimal (base 16) system also is used with computers.

The same mathematical principles apply to the decimal, binary, and hexadecimal number systems.

A. _____ [p. 3.22]

Uses 10 symbols

Each of the symbols in the number system has a value associated with it.

B. _____ [p. 3.23]

Uses two symbols (0 and 1)

Each position in a decimal number has a place value associated with it.

C. _____ [p. 3.24]

Uses 16 symbols

Also a positional number system

Used to represent binary values in a more compact form.

D. Summary of number systems [p. 3.24]

Binary is used to represent the electronic status of the bits in memory and storage.

Hexadecimal is used to represent binary in a more compact form.

XVIII. How computer chips are made [p. 3.25]

A computer chip is made _____

_____

Integrated circuits are _____

_____

Although other materials can be used, the most common raw material used to make chips is silicon crystals.

The silicon crystals are melted _____

After being smoothed, the silicon ingot _____

_____

A clean room is _____

People who work in these facilities must wear special protective clothing called bunny suits.

After cleaning, the wafers are _____

_____

Dopants are added _____

Channels in these layers _____

Before etching, a soft gelatin-like emulsion called photoresist is added to the wafer.

During photolithography, _____

_____

Ultraviolet light is used because its short wavelength can reproduce very small details on the wafer.

Up to 100 images of the chip design are exposed on a single wafer.

The soft photoresist and some of the surface materials _____

_____

In a process called dicing, _____

Die that have passed all tests are placed in a ceramic or plastic case called a package.

XIX. Summary of the system unit [p. 3.25]

Examined various aspects of the system unit including _____

Studied _____

TERMS

access speed [p. 3.13]
adapter cards [p. 3.15]
American Standard Code for Information Interchange (ASCII) [p. 3.4]
analog computers [p. 3.3]
arithmetic operations [p. 3.8]
arithmetic/logic unit (ALU) [p. 3.8]

bay [p. 3.18]
bit [p. 3.3]
bunny suits [p. 3.25]
bus [p. 3.14]
byte [p. 3.3]

cache [p. 3.12]
cage [p. 3.18]
central processing unit (CPU) [p. 3.8]
chip [p. 3.8]
CISC [p. 3.19]
clean rooms [p. 3.25]
CMOS (complementary metal-oxide semiconductor) [p. 3.13]
connectors [p. 3.16]
control unit [p. 3.8]
controller cards [p. 3.15]
coprocessor [p. 3.14]

decoding [p. 3.8]
dicing [p. 3.27]
die [p. 3.27]
diffusion oven [p. 3.26]
digital computers [p. 3.3]
digitizing [p. 3.3]
DIMM (dual in-line memory module) [p. 3.12]
dopants [p. 3.26]

drive bay [p. 3.18]
dynamic RAM (DRAM) [p. 3.13]
etching [p. 3.26]
even parity [p. 3.5]
executing [p. 3.8]
execution cycle [p. 3.8]
expansion board [p. 3.15]
expansion bus [p. 3.14]
expansion card [p. 3.15]
expansion slot [p. 3.15]
Extended Binary Coded Decimal Interchange Code (EBCDIC) [p. 3.4]

fetching [p. 3.8]
firmware [p. 3.13]
flash memory [p. 3.11]
flash RAM [p. 3.11]

gigabyte (GB) [p. 3.11]
gigaflops (GFLOPS) [p. 3.20]

hexadecimal [p. 3.22]

ideograms [p. 3.4]
instruction cycle [p. 3.8]
instruction set [p. 3.19]
integrated circuit (IC) [p. 3.8, 3.25]
interface cards [p. 3.15]
internal cache [p. 3.12]
ion implantation [p. 3.26]
kilobyte (K or KB) [p. 3.11]

level 1 (L1) cache [p. 3.12]
level 2 (L2) cache [p. 3.12]
local bus [p. 3.14]
logical operations [p. 3.8]

machine cycle [p. 3.8]
machine language instruction [p. 3.19]
main board [p. 3.7]
massively parallel processor (MPP) [p. 3.21]
megabyte (MB) [p. 3.11]
megaflops (MFLOPS) [p. 3.20]
megahertz (MHz) [p. 3.9]
memory [p. 3.11]
memory address [p. 3.11]
microcode [p. 3.13]
microprocessor [p. 3.7]
millisecond [p. 3.14]
MIPS [p. 3.20]
motherboard [p. 3.7]
musical instrument digital interface (MIDI) [p. 3.18]
nanoseconds [p. 3.13]
neural network computers [p. 3.22]
nonvolatile [p. 3.13]

odd parity [p. 3.5]
operand [p. 3.20]
operation code [p. 3.20]

package [p. 3.27]
parallel ports [p. 3.16]
parallel processing [p. 3.21]
parity bit [p. 3.5]
PC Card [p. 3.16]
PCMCIA [p. 3.16]
photolithography [p. 3.26]
photoresist [p. 3.26]
pipelining [p. 3.21]

(continued)

port [p. 3.16]
power supply [p. 3.18]
rails [p. 3.18]
RAM (random access memory) [p. 3.11]
registers [p. 3.8]
RISC [p. 3.19]
ROM (read only memory) [p. 3.13]

SCSI [p. 3.16]
serial port [p. 3.18]
SIMM (single in-line memory module) [p. 3.12]
sound board [p. 3.18]
static RAM (SRAM) [p. 3.13]
storing [p. 3.8]
superscalar CPUs [p. 3.21]
system board [p. 3.7]
system clock [p. 3.8]

system unit [p. 3.2]
Unicode [p. 3.4]
Universal Serial Bus (USB) [p. 3.18]
upgrade socket [p. 3.10]
volatile [p. 3.11]
wafers [p. 3.25]
word size [p. 3.9]

SELF TEST

True/False

_____ 1. Most computers are analog computers, designed to process continuously variable data.

_____ 2. The Extended Binary Coded Decimal Interchange Code, or EBCDIC, is the most widely used coding system to represent data.

_____ 3. The central processing unit (CPU) contains the control unit and the arithmetic/logic unit.

_____ 4. Memory refers to integrated circuits that permanently store program instructions and data that can be retrieved.

_____ 5. Cache that is not part of the CPU chip is called level 2 (L2) cache.

_____ 6. Ports have different types of couplers, called connectors, that are used to attach cables to peripheral devices.

_____ 7. The power supply converts the wall outlet electricity (115-120 volts AC) to the lower voltages (5 to 12 volts DC) used by the computer.

_____ 8. A machine language instruction is decimal data that the electronic circuits in the CPU can interpret and convert into one or more of the commands in the computer's instruction set.

_____ 9. Parallel processors require special software that can recognize how to divide up problems and bring the results back together again.

_____ 10. The most common raw material used to make chips is silicon crystals.

Matching

1. _____ analog computers
2. _____ parity bit
3. _____ machine cycle
4. _____ cache memory
5. _____ CMOS
6. _____ bus
7. _____ serial port
8. _____ instruction set
9. _____ massively parallel processors
10. _____ hexadecimal

a. fetching, decoding, executing, and storing

b. contains commands that the computer's circuits can directly perform

c. transmits data one bit at a time

d. base 16 number system commonly used with computers

e. stores information about the computer system

f. used by the computer for error checking

g. transfer eight bits (one byte) at a time

h. can be used to install more powerful CPUs or additional memory

i. any path along which bits are transmitted

j. all memory above 1MB, used for programs and data

k. small circuit board that holds multiple RAM chips

l. use hundreds of thousands of microprocessor CPUs to perform calculations

m. consists of 32MB of memory on a memory expansion board

n. designed to process continuously variable data

o. high-speed RAM memory between the CPU and the main RAM memory

Multiple Choice

1. In a group of eight bits, called a byte, how many different data possibilities can be represented by using all the combinations of 0s and 1s?
    a. 8
    b. 16
    c. 256
    d. 1,024

2. The Extended Binary Coded Decimal Interchange Code (EBCDIC) is used primarily on what category of computers?
    a. personal computers
    b. minicomputers
    c. mainframe computers
    d. all of the above

3. What is the motherboard?
    a. a circuit board that contains most of the electronic components of the system unit
    b. a single integrated circuit that contains the CPU or central processing unit
    c. a special microprocessor chip or circuit board designed to perform a specific task
    d. a temporary storage location for a specific type of data

4. During which operation in the machine cycle are program instructions translated into commands the computer can process?
    a. fetching
    b. decoding
    c. executing
    d. storing

5. Which of the following is *not* stored in RAM (random access memory)?
    a. the operating system and other system software that direct and coordinate hardware
    b. the application program instructions that direct the work to be done
    c. the data currently being processed by the application programs
    d. the startup instructions and data used when a computer is first turned on

6. Parallel ports often are used to connect which of the following devices?
    a. printers or disk and tape drives
    b. the keyboard or the mouse
    c. communications devices such as a modem
    d. an electronic keyboard or music synthesizer

(continued)

_____ 7. What is a bay?
   a. a path along which bits are transmitted
   b. a socket designed to hold the circuit board for a device
   c. a socket used to connect the system unit to a device
   d. an open area inside the system unit used to install additional equipment

_____ 8. What part of a machine language instruction tells the computer what to do and matches one of the commands in the instruction set?
   a. the firmware
   b. the operation code
   c. the microcode
   d. the operand

_____ 9. How does pipelining result in faster throughput?
   a. a new instruction is started as soon as the preceding instruction moves on to the next stage in the machine cycle
   b. a single instruction is processed at a time, and when that instruction is completely finished, the CPU begins execution of the next instruction
   c. problems are divided among multiple CPUs so each can work on its assigned portion of the problem simultaneously
   d. specially designed circuits are used to simulate the way the human brain processes information, learns, and remembers

_____ 10. What quantity is represented by binary 1011?
   a. decimal 7
   b. hexadecimal A
   c. decimal 11
   d. hexadecimal F

Fill in the Blanks

1. Converting data into digital form is called _____.

2. _____ is the coding system used on personal computers and minicomputers.

3. In computers with _____, the total number of *on* bits must be a number divisible by 2.

4. Components considered part of the _____ include the motherboard, microprocessor and CPU, memory, ports and connectors, and the power supply.

5. In the machine cycle, _____ takes place when the result of the instruction is written to memory.

6. The _____ is the number of bits the CPU processes at one time.

7. ROM memory is described as _____ because it retains its contents even when the power is turned off.

8. A(n) _____ is a special type of parallel port that can be used to attach seven to fifteen different devices to a single port.

9. Some manufacturers have designed CPUs based on _____ technology, which involves reducing the instructions in the instruction set to only those that are most frequently used.

10. After being smoothed, the silicon ingot is sliced into _____ four to eight inches in diameter.

Complete the Table

Name	Date	Manufacturer	Word Size	Bus Width	Clock Speed (MHz)	MIPS
_____	1995	Intel	64	_____	_____	300
Pentium	1993	_____	_____	64	75-166	_____
_____	1989	Intel	32	32	_____	20-___
80386DX	_____	Intel	_____	32	16-33	6-12
_____	1994	Motorola	64	_____	_____	300
Alpha	1993	_____	64	64	150-____	_____

Things to Think About

1. How does a coding system make it possible for different computers to share data?

2. Why are the first two operations in the machine cycle, fetching and decoding, called the instruction cycle? Why are the last two operations, executing and storing, called the execution cycle?

3. Why do special-purpose computers, such as those used in automobiles or appliances, use ROM memory instead of RAM memory?

4. Why are connectors designed in a variety of shapes? Why are they frequently asymmetrical?

5. If, according to Moore's Law, transistor density doubles every 18 to 24 months, will transistor technology ever reach a point where it can become no smaller?

Puzzle

Write the word described by each clue in the puzzle below. Words can be written forward or backward, across, up and down, or diagonally. The initial letter of each word already appears in the puzzle.

							O	C		A
M										
					C		E			
			M	R						B
D										
			S			M				
A				B						
		C				B				
					L					
					D					
F							B		C	
			L							P

because most computers are this type, the data they process must first be converted into a numeric value

smallest unit of data handled by a computer

a group of eight bits

most widely used coding system to represent data

coding system used primarily on mainframe computers

in computers with this, the total number of *on* bits in a byte must be an odd number

contains the control unit and the arithmetic/logic unit

can be thought of as the *brain* of the computer

machine cycle operation referring to the actual processing of the computer commands

contains the electronic circuitry necessary to perform arithmetic and logical operations on data

type of operations that consist of comparing one data item to another

name given to the integrated circuits, or chips, that are used for main memory

approximately one million bytes

today, most RAM memory is installed by using this

type of RAM chips that comprise memory, with access speeds of 50 to 100 nanoseconds

instructions stored in ROM memory

a special microprocessor chip or circuit board designed to perform a specific task

any path along which bits can be transmitted

an expansion bus that connects directly to the CPU is called this type of bus

type of cards used for additional memory, storage, and communications

type of ports that can transfer eight bits (one byte) at a time

type of serial port designed to be connected to a musical device

an open area inside the system unit used to install additional equipment

two or more bays side by side or on top of one another

part of a machine language instruction that specifies the data or the location of the data that will be used

type of computers with hundreds of commands in their instruction sets

one million instructions per second

SELF TEST ANSWERS

True/False
1. *F* [p. 3.3]
2. *F* [p. 3.4]
3. *T* [p. 3.8]
4. *F* [p. 3.11]
5. *T* [p. 3.12]
6. *T* [p. 3.16]
7. *T* [p. 3.18]
8. *F* [p. 3.19]
9. *T* [p. 3.21]
10. *T* [p. 3.25]

Matching
1. *n* [p. 3.3]
2. *f* [p. 3.5]
3. *a* [p. 3.8]
4. *o* [p. 3.12]
5. *e* [p. 3.13]
6. *i* [p. 3.14]
7. *c* [p. 3.18]
8. *b* [p. 3.19]
9. *l* [p. 3.21]
10. *d* [p. 3.24]

Multiple Choice
1. *c* [p. 3.3]
2. *c* [p. 3.4]
3. *a* [p. 3.7]
4. *b* [p. 3.8]
5. *d* [p. 3.13]
6. *a* [p. 3.16]
7. *d* [p. 3.18]
8. *b* [p. 3.20]
9. *a* [p. 3.21]
10. *c* [p. 3.22]

Fill in the Blanks
1. *digitizing* [p. 3.3]
2. *ASCII* [p. 3.4]
3. *even parity* [p. 3.5]
4. *system unit* [p. 3.6]
5. *storing* [p. 3.8]
6. *word size* [p. 3.9]
7. *nonvolatile* [p. 3.13]
8. *SCSI port* [p. 3.16]
9. *RISC* [p. 3.19]
10. *wafers* [p. 3.25]

Complete the Table [p. 3.10]

Name	Date	Manufacturer	Word Size	Bus Width	Clock Speed (MHz)	MIPS
Pentium Pro	1995	Intel	64	*64*	*150-200*	300
Pentium	1993	*Intel*	*64*	64	75-166	*150*
80486DX	1989	Intel	32	32	*25-100*	20-*75*
80386DX	*1985*	Intel	*32*	32	16-33	6-12
PowerPC	1994	Motorola	64	*64*	*50-225*	300
Alpha	1993	*Digital*	64	64	150-*333*	*275-1332*

Puzzle Answer

Y	T	I	R	A	P	D	D	**O**	**C**	**T**	**A**
M	E	G	A	B	Y	T	E	P	O	I	L
G	N	I	T	U	**C**	E	X	**E**	P	N	U
S	P	I	**M**	A	**R**	P	B	R	R	U	**B**
D	Y	N	A	M	I	C	U	A	O	L	U
M	M	I	**S**	I	D	I	**M**	N	C	O	S
A	S	C	I	**B**	I	T	D	E	R	A
E	G	A	**C**	I	S	C	**B**	E	S	T	I
L	A	C	I	G	O	**L**	A	T	S	N	C
L	A	T	I	G	I	**D**	Y	Y	O	O	M
F	I	R	M	W	A	R	E	**B**	R	**C**	C
L	A	C	O	**L**	E	L	L	A	R	A	**P**

CHAPTER 4
Input and Output

CHAPTER OVERVIEW

This chapter discusses and describes some of the devices used for input and output. The chapter begins with an overview of input. Input is defined, and the four types of input are explained. You discover how the keyboard and various pointing devices are used to input data. Source data automation is defined, and the equipment used for source data collection is described. You learn about terminals and different types of multimedia input devices. The chapter then turns the discussion to output. Output is defined, and various types of output are described. You learn how printers are classified, the characteristics of several kinds of impact and nonimpact printers, other types of printers developed for special purposes, and considerations in choosing a printer. Display devices are characterized and explained. Finally, other output devices available for particular uses and applications, including data projectors, plotters, computer output microfilm, and voice output, are described.

CHAPTER OBJECTIVES

After completing this chapter, you will be able to:

- Define the four types of input and how the computer uses each type
- Describe the standard features of keyboards and explain how to use the arrow and function keys
- Explain how a mouse and other pointing devices work and how they are used
- Describe several different methods of source data automation
- Define the term output
- Describe different types of printed output
- Identify different types of display devices
- Explain the difference between impact and nonimpact printers
- Explain how images are displayed on a screen
- List and describe other types of output devices used with computers

CHAPTER OUTLINE

I. What is input? [p. 4.2]

Input refers to _____

_____

(continued)

Four types of input:

- Data refers to _____

- Programs are _____

- Commands are _____

- User responses refer to _____

II. The keyboard [p. 4.2]

Most commonly used input device

Connected to other devices that have screens to display data as it is entered

Keyboard components:

Alphabetic keys arranged like _____

Numeric keypad is _____

Keys that can move the insertion point _____

An insertion point, or cursor, is a symbol _____

_____

Keys that can alter or edit the text: _____

The CAPS LOCK key is an example _____

Function keys are _____

Status lights indicate _____

The ESCAPE (ESC) key often is used by _____

The disadvantage of using a keyboard is _____

III. Pointing devices [p. 4.5]

Used to control an on-screen symbol, called the mouse pointer or pointer

Usually is represented by _____

A. Mouse [p. 4.5]

A mouse is _____

_____

By clicking the buttons on the mouse, you can perform actions such as _____,

_____, _____, and _____, or

_____

To press and release the mouse button twice _____

The primary advantage of a mouse is _____

Disadvantages of a mouse are _____

_____

B. Trackball [p. 4.6]

A trackball is _____

The main advantage of a trackball over a mouse is _____

C. Touchpad [p. 4.6]

A touchpad, sometimes called a trackpad, is a flat rectangular surface _____

_____

Touchpads often are built into portable computers

D. Pointing stick [p. 4.7]

Sometimes called a _____

_____

Used on portable computers because they require little space

Another advantage _____

E. Joystick [p. 4.7]

A joystick uses _____

F. Pen input [p. 4.8]

Increasingly popular, used with almost all personal digital assistants (PDAs)

Pen input devices can be used in three ways: _____

_____

The darkened area on the screen _____

Hand-written characters are converted into computer text by _____

_____

Most handwriting recognition software can be taught to recognize an individual's unique style of writing.

Pressing the pen against the screen _____

_____

Gestures are _____

Pen input devices already have been adapted _____

_____

G. Touch screen [p. 4.9]

Allows users to _____

Used for _____

H. Light pen [p. 4.10]

A light pen is _____

I. Digitizer [p. 4.10]

A digitizer converts _____

J. Graphics tablet [p. 4.11]

A graphics tablet works _____

IV. Source data automation [p. 4.12]

Also known as source data collection

Refers to _____

Original form from which data is collected is called a source document.

A. Image scanner [p. 4.13]

An image scanner, sometimes called a page scanner, is _____

_____

Image processing systems use _____

(continued)

B. Optical recognition [p. 4.14]

Optical recognition devices use _____

_____

    1.   Optical codes [p. 4.14]

        Use a pattern or symbol to represent data

        A bar code, the most common optical code, consists of _____

        _____

        Most familiar bar code is the _____

    2.   Optical mark recognition (OMR) [p. 4.15]

        OMR devices often are _____

    3.   Optical character recognition (OCR) [p. 4.15]

        OCR devices are _____

        Scans the shape of a character _____

        Frequently used for turn-around documents designed to be returned to the organization that created them

    4.   OCR software [p. 4.16]

        Used with _____

        _____

C. _____ [p. 4.17]

MICR characters use a special ink that can be magnetized during processing.

Used almost exclusively by _____

D. Data collection devices [p. 4.17]

Designed and used for _____

_____

V. Terminals [p. 4.18]

Sometimes called display terminals or video display terminals (VDTs), consist of _____

_____

A dumb terminal consists of _____

_____

A dumb terminal has no independent processing capability or secondary storage and cannot function as an independent device.

Intelligent terminals have _____

_____

Intelligent terminals also are known as _____

_____

Special-purpose terminals perform specific jobs and contain features uniquely designed for use in a particular industry.

Point-of-sale (POS) terminals are special-purpose terminals that allow _____

_____

ATMs are another kind of _____

_____

VI. Other input devices [p. 4.19]

The use of sound and image data is increasing, and to capture sound and image data requires special input devices and cards that convert the input into a digital form that can be stored and processed by the computer.

A. Sound input [p. 4.19]

_____

_____

B. Voice input [p. 4.19]

Sometimes referred to as speech or voice recognition.

Digital signal processing (DSP) converts _____

Speaker dependent voice input systems require _____

_____

Voice templates are used when _____

The use of voice templates make a system speaker independent.

Discrete-speech recognition requires _____

Continuous-speech recognition allows _____

A natural language voice interface allows _____

_____

C. Biological feedback input [p. 4.21]

Devices work in combination with _____

_____

D. Digital camera [p. 4.21]

Records photographs in the form of _____

E. Video input [p. 4.22]

Video material is input to the computer _____

Requires tremendous amounts of storage space

F. Electronic whiteboards [p. 4.22]

Is a _____

_____

VII. What is output? [p. 4.23]

Output is _____

_____

VIII. Types of output [p. 4.23]

Two common types of output are _____

Output that is printed is called _____

Output that is displayed on a screen is called _____

A. Reports [p. 4.23]

A report is _____

Reports also can be classified by who uses them:

An internal report is used by _____

(continued)

An external report is used by _____

Reports can be classified by the way they present information:

Narrative reports are _____

In a detail report, _____

A summary report _____

An exception report _____

Reports can be classified by how often they are produced:

Periodic reports (scheduled reports) are produced _____

Ad-hoc (on-demand) reports are created _____

   B.   Graphics [p. 4.25]

      Computer graphics are _____

      Computer drawing programs and computer paint programs allow an artistic user to create stunning works of art.

   C.   Audio output [p. 4.25]

      Audio output, consists of _____

      Voice output is _____

      _____

      Data that produces voice output usually is created in one of two ways.

      First, a person can talk into a device _____

      _____

      Second, voice synthesis _____

      _____

   D.   Video output [p. 4.26]

      Video output consists of _____

      _____

      High-definition television (HDTV) sets are _____

IX.   Display devices [p. 4.27]

   A display device is _____

   The two most common types of display devices _____

   A.   Monitors [p. 4.27]

      A monitor looks _____

      The term screen is used to refer to both the surface of any display device and to any type of display device.

      A CRT (cathode ray tube) is _____

      Color monitors can display text or graphics in color.

      Maximum number of colors _____

      Monochrome monitors display _____

      Monachrome monitors are still used by _____

      Gray scaling involves _____

   B.   Flat panel displays [p. 4.29]

A flat panel display is _____

_____

Use two common types of technology _____
In a liquid crystal display (LCD) _____

_____

Active matrix LCD screens use _____
Passive matrix LCD screens use _____
Dual scan _____
Gas plasma screens _____

C. Resolution [p. 4.30]

Images are displayed on a monitor using patterns of lighted dots.

A picture element, or pixel, is each dot that can be lighted.

Resolution, or clarity, of an image is directly related _____

_____

Dot pitch is _____

Monitors and video adapter cards often are identified by the highest graphics display standard they support.

Video graphics standards include: _____

Multiscanning (multisync) monitors, designed to work within a range of frequencies, can work with different standards and video adapters.

D. How images are displayed on a monitor [p. 4.31]

1. Image sent electronically from CPU to video circuits in CRT.
2. _____

_____

The screen is coated with colored phosphorus dots, which glow when struck by the electron beam.

3. Yoke moves electron beam across and down screen.

Interlaced monitors _____
Noninterlaced monitors _____

Refresh rate is speed at which entire screen is redrawn.

4. _____

X. Printers [p. 4.32]

Different needs have resulted in the development of printers with varying speeds, capabilities, and printing methods.

Generally, printers can be classified _____

A. Impact printers [p. 4.32]

Transfer the image onto paper by _____

_____

Most use continuous-form paper, with the pages connected together for a continuous flow through the printer

1. Dot matrix printers [p. 4.32]

Produce printed images by _____

(continued)

Speed rated in _____

_____

Although inexpensive, they are less frequently used.

Often are used _____

Dot matrix printers range in cost from _____

   2. Band printers [p. 4.34]

Used for high-volume output on large computer systems

Band printers use _____

B. Nonimpact printers [p. 4.34]

Nonimpact printing means _____

   1. Ink-jet printers [p. 4.34]

Sprays _____

Produce high-quality print and graphics and are quiet

   2. Laser printers [p. 4.36]

Similar to a copy machine

Data from the computer is converted _____

_____

Some laser-type printers use _____

All produce high-quality text and graphics suitable for business correspondence

Speed is measured in _____

Resolution is measured by _____

   3. Thermal printers [p. 4.37]

Thermal printers (thermal transfer printers) use _____

_____

A special type of thermal printer, using a method called dye diffusion, uses chemically treated paper to obtain color print quality equal to glossy magazine pages.

Produce output at a rate of _____

C. Plotters [p. 4.38]

A plotter is _____

Pen plotters _____

Two kinds of pen plotters are:

_____ – _____

_____ – _____

An electrostatic plotter _____

D. Special-purpose printers [p. 4.39]

Printers developed for special purposes include _____

_____

XI. Other output devices [p. 4.40]

Other output devices are available for particular uses and applications.

A. Data projectors [p. 4.40]

Project the image on a computer screen for a room full of people

LCD projection panels _____

_____

Self-contained LCD projectors have their own source of light

The three-beam projectors _____

B. Computer output microfilm [p. 4.41]

Computer output microfilm (COM) is _____

Information recorded on sheet film called microfiche

Advantages of microfilm over printed reports: _____

_____

_____

Some microfilm readers can perform automatic data lookup called computer-assisted retrieval (CAR).

C. Facsimile (Fax) [p. 4.42]

Used to _____

_____

Stand-alone fax _____

Internal fax _____

_____

D. Multifunction devices [p. 4.42]

A single piece of equipment that can print, scan, copy, and fax.

Two primary advantages: _____

_____

Obvious risk in using multifunction devices is _____

XII. Summary of input and output [p. 4.43]

The input and output steps _____

TERMS

active matrix [p. 4.29]
arrow control keys [p. 4.3]
arrow keys [p. 4.3]
audio output [p. 4.25]

band printer [p. 4.34]
bar code [p. 4.14]
biological feedback input
  [p. 4.21]
cathode ray tube (CRT) [p. 4.27]
characters per second (cps)
  [p. 4.33]
clicking [p. 4.5]
color monitor [p. 4.28]
commands [p. 4.2]
computer-assisted retrieval (CAR)
  [p. 4.41]

computer drawing programs
  [p. 4.25]
computer graphics [p. 4.25]
computer output microfilm
  (COM) [p. 4.41]
computer paint programs
  [p. 4.25]
continuous-speech recognition
  [p. 4.20]
continuous-form paper [p. 4.32]
CRT (cathode ray tube) [p. 4.27]
cursor [p. 4.3]

data [p. 4.2]
data collection devices [p. 4.17]
detail report [p. 4.23]
digital cameras [p. 4.21]
digitizer [p. 4.10]

discrete-speech recognition
  [p. 4.20]
display terminals [p. 4.18]
dot matrix printer [p. 4.32]
dots per inch (dpi) [p. 4.37]
double-clicking [p. 4.5]
dragging [p. 4.5]
drum plotter [p. 4.38]
dual scan [p. 4.29]
dumb terminal [p. 4.18]
dye diffusion [p. 4.37]

electronic whiteboard [p. 4.22]
electrostatic plotter [p. 4.39]
exception report [p. 4.24]
external report [p. 4.23]

(continued)

facsimile [p. 4.42]
fax [p. 4.42]
flat panel display [p. 4.29]
flatbed plotter [p. 4.38]
function keys [p. 4.4]

gas plasma [p. 4.29]
gestures [p. 4.8]
graphics tablet [p. 4.11]

hard copy [p. 4.23]
high-definition television (HDTV) [p. 4.26]

image processing systems [p. 4.13]
image scanner [p. 4.13]
impact printers [p. 4.32]
ink [p. 4.8]
ink-jet printer [p. 4.34]
input [p. 4.2]
insertion point [p. 4.3]
intelligent terminals [p. 4.18]
interlaced monitors [p. 4.31]
internal report [p. 4.23]

joystick [p. 4.7]

keyboard [p. 4.2]

laser printer [p. 4.36]
LCD projection panels [p. 4.40]
LCD projectors [p. 4.40]
light pen [p. 4.10]
lines per minute (lpm) [p. 4.33]
liquid crystal display (LCD) [p. 4.29]

magnetic ink character recognition (MICR) [p. 4.17]
microfiche [p. 4.41]
monitor [p. 4.27]
monochrome monitors [p. 4.28]

mouse [p. 4.5]
mouse pad [p. 4.5]
mouse pointer [p. 4.5]
multifunction device (MFD) [p. 4.42]
multiscanning monitors [p. 4.30]
multisync monitors [p. 4.30]

narrative report [p. 4.23]
nonimpact printing [p. 4.34]
noninterlaced monitors [p. 4.31]
numeric keypad [p. 4.3]

OCR software [p. 4.16]
on-demand report [p. 4.24]
optical character recognition (OCR) [p. 4.15]
optical codes [p. 4.14]
optical mark recognition (OMR) [p. 4.15]
optical recognition [p. 4.14]
output [p. 4.23]

page scanner [p. 4.13]
pages per minute (ppm) [p. 4.37]
passive matrix [p. 4.29]
pen input [p. 4.8]
pen plotter [p. 4.38]
periodic report [p. 4.24]
picture element [p. 4.30]
pixel [p. 4.30]
plotter [p. 4.38]
pointer [p. 4.5]
pointing stick [p. 4.7]
point-of-sale (POS) terminal [p. 4.18]
programmable terminal [p. 4.18]
programs [p. 4.2]

refresh rate [p. 4.31]
report [p. 4.23]

resolution [p. 4.30]
scheduled reports [p. 4.24]
screen [p. 4.27]
smart terminal [p. 4.18]
soft copy [p. 4.23]
sound card [p. 4.19]
source data automation [p. 4.12]
source data collection [p. 4.12]
source document [p. 4.12]
special-purpose terminal [p. 4.18]
summary report [p. 4.24]
SVGA [p. 4.30]

terminals [p. 4.18]
thermal printer [p. 4.37]
thermal transfer printers [p. 4.37]
toggle key [p. 4.3]
touch screen [p. 4.9]
touchpad [p. 4.6]
trackball [p. 4.6]
trackpad [p. 4.6]
trackpoint [p. 4.7]
turn-around documents [p. 4.16]

universal product code (UPC) [p. 4.14]
user responses [p. 4.2]

VGA (video graphics array) [p. 4.30]
video card [p. 4.19]
video display terminals (VDTs) [p. 4.18]
video input [p. 4.22]
video output [p. 4.26]
voice input [p. 4.19]
voice output [p. 4.26]
voice synthesis [p. 4.26]
voice templates [p. 4.20]

SELF TEST
True/False

_____ 1. The advantage of using a keyboard as an input device is that little training is required to use it efficiently.

_____ 2. Most handwriting recognition software can be taught to recognize an individual's unique style of writing.

_____ 3. Pen input devices already have been adapted to many applications that were previously not computerized.

_____ 4. Touch screens are not used to enter large amounts of data.

_____ 5. The characters in the standard OCR typeface, called OCR-A, are easily read by machines but cannot be read by people.

_____ 6. An exception report contains information that is outside of normal user-specified values or conditions, called the exception criteria.

_____ 7. Voice synthesis can transform words stored in memory into speech.

_____ 8. The distance between each pixel is called the resolution.

_____ 9. Laser printers spray tiny drops of toner onto the paper.

_____ 10. Drum plotters use a rotary drum, or cylinder, over which drawing pens are mounted; the pens move left and right as the drum rotates.

Matching

1. _____ function keys

2. _____ light pen

3. _____ optical codes

4. _____ data collection device

5. _____ speaker independent

6. _____ periodic report

7. _____ audio output

8. _____ flat panel display

9. _____ ink-jet printer

10. _____ COM

a. the most commonly used input device

b. technique that records output as microscopic images on roll or sheet film

c. used by touching it on the display screen to create or modify graphics

d. designed and used for obtaining data at the site where the transaction or event being reported takes place

e. use a special ink that is magnetized during processing

f. programmed to initiate commands and accomplish certain tasks

g. used with image scanners to convert text images into data that can be processed

h. use a pattern or symbols to represent data

i. contains a nozzle with holes that sprays tiny drops of ink onto the paper

j. consists of sounds, including words and music, produced by the computer

k. voice input systems that do not have to be trained to the user's speech patterns

l. works in a manner similar to a digitizer but also contains unique characters and commands

m. require the user to pause slightly between each word

n. screen that does not use cathode ray tube (CRT) technology

o. produced on a regular basis such as daily, weekly, monthly, or yearly

Multiple Choice

1. User responses are one type of input used by a computer. What are user responses?
   a. raw facts, including numbers, letters, words, images, and sounds that a computer processes to produce information
   b. instructions that direct the computer to perform the necessary operations to process data into information
   c. key words and phrases that the user inputs to direct the computer to perform certain activities
   d. data a user inputs to respond to a question or message from the software

2. What is an insertion point or cursor?
   a. a symbol that indicates where on the screen the next character entered will appear
   b. a set of numeric keys move the insertion point around the screen
   c. a set of keys located at the top of the keyboard
   d. a symbol the mouse pointer becomes while waiting for the user to enter data

3. Which of the following is *not* used in source data automation?
   a. graphics tablet
   b. image scanner
   c. magnetic ink character recognition
   d. optical recognition device

4. How are intelligent terminals different from dumb terminals?
   a. an intelligent terminal consists of a keyboard and a display screen that are used to enter and transmit data to or receive and display data from a computer to which it is connected
   b. an intelligent terminal has no secondary storage and cannot function as a stand-alone device
   c. an intelligent terminal allows data to be entered at the time and place where a transaction with a customer occurs
   d. an intelligent terminal can perform limited processing tasks when it is not communicating directly with the central computer

5. What type of voice input system uses voice templates?
   a. speaker dependent
   b. speaker independent
   c. discrete speech recognition
   d. digital signal processing

6. What is soft copy output?
   a. output that is displayed on a screen
   b. output that is printed on paper
   c. output that has been saved on a floppy disk
   d. output that simulates a three-dimensional environment

7. What type of report is primarily text-based?
   a. narrative
   b. detail
   c. summary
   d. all of the above

_____ 8. What type of monitor is designed to work within a range of frequencies and thus can work with different standards and video adapters?

    a.   VGA

    b.   interlaced

    c.   multisync

    d.   noninterlaced

_____ 9. Into what two groups are printers generally classified?

    a.   tractor feed or friction feed, based on how paper is transported through the printer

    b.   impact or nonimpact, based on how characters are transferred to the paper

    c.   unidirectional or bi-directional, based on the movement of the print head

    d.   draft quality or letter quality, based on the appearance of the printed output

_____ 10. What is a plotter?

    a.   an output device designed to be placed on top of an overhead projector

    b.   an output device used to produce high-quality line drawings

    c.   an output device that records output as microscopic images on sheet film

    d.   an output device that can transform words stored in main memory into speech

Fill in the Blanks

1. _____, one type of input used by a computer, are instructions that direct the computer to perform the operations necessary to process data into information.

2. A(n) _____ is a small, lightweight input device that is moved across a flat surface to control the movement of the pointer on the screen.

3. _____ can be used in three ways: to input data using hand-written characters and shapes the computer can recognize, as a pointing device to select items on the screen, and to gesture, which is a way of issuing commands.

4. _____ devices use a light source to read codes, marks, and characters and convert them into digital data that can be processed by a computer.

5. _____ terminals allow data to be entered at the time and place where the transaction with a customer occurs.

6. In a(n) _____, each line on the report usually corresponds to one record that has been processed.

7. _____ can transform words stored in memory into speech.

8. Gas plasma screens substitute an _____ for the liquid crystal material.

9. _____ illuminate every other line on the screen and then return to the top to illuminate the lines they skipped.

10. _____, which take the image that displays on a computer screen and project it so it can be clearly seen by a room full of people, use liquid crystal display technology and are designed to be placed on top of an overhead projector.

Complete the Table

INPUT DEVICE	DESCRIPTION
Keyboard	Most commonly used input device; special keys may include numeric keypad, arrow keys, and function keys
Mouse, Trackball, Touchpad, Pointing Stick	_____
_____	Stem device often used as input device for games
Touch Screen	_____
_____	Used to enter or edit drawings
Graphics Tablet	_____
_____	Converts text, graphics, or photos into digital input
MICR	_____
_____	Captures digital image of subject or object
Video Input	_____

Complete the Table

OUTPUT DEVICE	DESCRIPTION
Printers – Impact	
Dot matrix	_____
_____	High-speed rotating band text-only printer.
Printers – Nonimpact	
Ink-jet	_____
_____	Works like a copying machine; produces very high quality text and graphics
Display Devices	
Monitor	_____
Flat panel display	_____
_____	Projects display screen image to a group
_____	Stores reduced-size image on sheet or roll film
Multifunction Devices	_____

Things to Think About

1. Why must the input operation take place before any other operation in the information processing cycle?

2. Four types of input are data, programs, commands, and user responses. What type of input devices (keyboard, pointing devices, source data automation equipment, or multimedia input devices) can be used to enter each type of input?

3. When might a company prefer having a dumb terminal to having a smart terminal? Why?

4. Why is output printed on paper, which is a flexible material, called hard copy while output displayed on a screen, which is firm to the touch, called soft copy?

5. Reports can be classified by who uses them, the way they present information, and how often they are produced. Is any type of report necessarily classified in a certain way? That is, are all detail reports also internal and/or periodic reports? Are any report classifications mutually exclusive (can an exception report also be an external or an on-demand report)? Why?

6. Does any type of report require a specific kind of printer or display device? Is any printer or display device inadequate for certain types of reports? Why?

Puzzle

The terms described by each phrase below are written in code. Break the code by writing the correct term above the coded word. Then, use your broken code to translate the final sentence.

1. the most commonly used input device

    $\kappa\varepsilon\psi\beta o\alpha\rho\delta$

2. allows users to touch areas of the screen to enter data

    $\tau o\upsilon\chi\eta\ \sigma\chi\rho\varepsilon\varepsilon\nu$

3. consists of a set of vertical lines and spaces of different widths

    $\beta\alpha\rho\ \chi o\delta\varepsilon$

4. type of documents designed to be returned

    $\tau\upsilon\rho\nu-\alpha\rho o\upsilon\nu\delta$

5. on-screen symbol usually represented by an arrow shape

    $\pi o\iota\nu\tau\varepsilon\rho$

6. flat rectangular surface that senses the movement of a finder on it surface

    $\tau o\upsilon\chi\eta\pi\alpha\delta$

7. symbols made with a pen input device that issue commands

    $\gamma\varepsilon\sigma\tau\upsilon\rho\varepsilon\sigma$

8. process of entering data into main memory

    $\iota\nu\pi\upsilon\tau$

9. indicates where the next character entered will appear

    $\chi\upsilon\rho\sigma o\rho$

(continued)

10. keys that move the cursor

αρροω

11. darkened area touched by the pen on a computer screen

ινκ

12. records photographs in the form of digital data

διγιταλ χαμερα

13. raw facts that a computer receives during the input operation

δατα

14. the combination of sound and images with text and graphics

μυλτιμεδια

15. original form in source data automation

σουρχε δοχυμεντ

16. input device that electronically captures an entire page

ιμαγε σχαννερ

17. terminal with no independent processing capability

δυμβ

18. input device often used with computer games

φοψστιχκ

19. can be programmed to accomplish certain tasks

φυνχτιον κεψσ

Τψπιστσ υσινγ τηε Μολτρον κεψβοαρδ, ωηιχη ισ σπλιτ ανδ χοντουρεδ το φιτ εαχη

ηανδ ωιτη τηε μοστ χομμονλψ υσεδ κεψσ υνδερ τηε στρονγεστ φινγερσ, χαν τψπε μορε

τηαν τηρεε τιμεσ φαστερ τηαν τψπιστσ υσινγ α τραδιτιοναλ κεψβοαρδ.

SELF TEST ANSWERS

True/False
1. F [p. 4.4]
2. T [p. 4.8]
3. T [p. 4.8]
4. T [p. 4.9]
5. F [p. 4.15]
6. T [p. 4.24]
7. T [p. 4.26]
8. F [p. 4.30]
9. F [p. 4.36]
10. T [p. 4.38]

Matching
1. f [p. 4.4]
2. c [p. 4.10]
3. h [p. 4.14]
4. d [p. 4.17]
5. k [p. 4.20]
6. o [p. 4.24]
7. j [p. 4.25]
8. n [p. 4.29]
9. i [p. 4.34]
10. b [p. 4.41]

Multiple Choice
1. d [p. 4.2]
2. a [p. 4.3]
3. a [p. 4.11]
4. d [p. 4.18]
5. b [p. 4.20]
6. a [p. 4.23]
7. a [p. 4.23]
8. c [p. 4.30]
9. b [p. 4.32]
10. b [p. 4.38]

Fill in the Blanks
1. Programs [p. 4.2]
2. mouse [p. 4.5]
3. Pen input devices [p. 4.8]
4. Optical recognition [p. 4.14]
5. Point-of-sale (POS) [p. 4.18]
6. detail report [p. 4.23]
7. Voice synthesis [p. 4.26]
8. neon gas [p. 4.29]
9. Interlaced monitors [p. 4.31]
10. LCD projection panels [p. 4.40]

Complete the Table [p. 4.22]

INPUT DEVICE	DESCRIPTION
Keyboard	Most commonly used input device; special keys may include numeric keypad, arrow keys, and function keys
Mouse, Trackball, Touchpad, Pointing Stick	*Used to move pointer and select options*
Joystick	Stem device often used as input device for games
Touch Screen	*User interacts with computer by touching screen with finger*
Digitizer	Used to enter or edit drawings
Graphics Tablet	*Digitizer with special processing options built into tablet*
Image Scanner	Converts text, graphics, or photos into digital input
MICR	*Used in banking to read magnetic ink characters on checks*
Digital Camera	Captures digital image of subject or object
Video Input	*Converts video into digital data*

Complete the Table [p. 4.43]

OUTPUT DEVICE	DESCRIPTION
Printers – Impact	
Dot matrix	*Prints text and graphics using small dots*
Band	High-speed rotating band text-only printer.
Printers – Nonimpact	
Ink-jet	*Sprays tiny drops of ink onto page to form text and graphics; prints quietly; inexpensive color printer*
Laser	Works like a copying machine; produces very high quality text and graphics
Display Devices	
Monitor	*Visual display like TV set*
Flat panel display	*Flat visual display used with portable computers*
Data Projectors	Projects display screen image to a group
COM	Stores reduced-size image on sheet or roll film
Multifunction Devices	*Combines printer, fax, scanner, and copier*

Puzzle Answer

1. the most commonly used input device

keyboard
κεψβοαρδ

2. allows users to touch areas of the screen to enter data

touch screen
τουχη σχρεεν

3. consists of a set of vertical lines and spaces of different widths

bar code
βαρ χοδε

4. type of documents designed to be returned

turn-around
τυρν−αρουνδ

5. on-screen symbol usually represented by an arrow-shape

pointer
ποιντερ

6. flat rectangular surface that senses the movement of a finder on it surface

touchpad
τουχηπαδ

7. symbols made with a pen input device that issue commands

gestures
γεστυρεσ

8. process of entering data into main memory

input
ινπυτ

9. indicates where the next character entered will appear

cursor
χυρσορ

10. keys that move the insertion point

arrow
αρροω

11. darkened area touched by the pen on a computer screen

ink
ινκ

12. records photographs in the form of digital data

digital camera
διγιταλ χαμερα

13. raw facts that a computer receives during the input operation

data
δατα

14. designed to work within a range of frequencies

multisync
μυλτισψνχ

15. original form in source data automation

source document
σουρχε δοχυμεντ

16. input device that electronically captures an entire page

image scanner
ιμαγε σχαννερ

17. terminal with no independent processing capability

dumb
δυμβ

(continued)

18. input device often used with computer games

joystick

φοψστιχκ

19. keys that can be programmed to accomplish certain tasks

function keys

φυνχτιον κεψσ

Typists using the Moltron keyboard, which is split and contoured to fit each

Τψπιστσ υσινγ τηε Μολτρον κεψβοαρδ, ωηιχη ισ σπλιτ ανδ χοντουρεδ το φιτ εαχη

hand with the more commonly used keys under the strongest fingers, can type more

ηανδ ωιτη τηε μορε χομμονλψ υσεδ κεψσ υνδερ τηε στρονγεστ φινγερσ, χαν τψπε μορε

than three times faster than typists using a traditional keyboard.

τηαν τηρεε τιμεσ φαστερ τηαν τψπιστσ υσινγ α τραδιτιοναλ κεψβοαρδ.

DISCOVERING COMPUTERS
A LINK TO THE FUTURE
WORLD WIDE WEB ENHANCED

C H A P T E R   5
Data Storage

CHAPTER OVERVIEW

This chapter explains storage operations and the various types of data storage devices that are used with computers. After storage is defined, magnetic disk storage is explored. You learn about floppy disks, hard disks, data compression, disk cartridges, and maintaining data stored on disks. The use of CD-ROM and optical disks is presented, followed by the use of magnetic tape storage. Finally, other forms of storage are examined, including PC Cards, RAID storage systems, mass storage devices, and special-purpose devices such as smart cards.

CHAPTER OBJECTIVES

After completing this chapter, you will be able to:

- Define storage

- Identify the major storage devices

- Explain how data is stored on floppy disks and hard disks

- Explain how data compression works

- Explain how data is stored on optical disks such as CD-ROMs

- Explain how magnetic tape storage is used with computers

- Describe other forms of storage: PC Cards, RAID, and mass storage devices

- Describe how special-purpose storage devices such as smart cards are used

CHAPTER OUTLINE

I. What is storage? [p. 5.2]

Storage (secondary storage or auxiliary storage) stores _____

Storage devices provide a more permanent form of storage than memory because _____

_____

The process of storing _____

(continued)

The process of retrieving _____

Storage devices also can be used as both input and output devices.

II. Magnetic disk storage [p. 5.3]

Most widely used storage medium for all types of computers

A magnetic disk consists _____

Types of magnetic disks include _____

A. Floppy disk [p. 5.3]

Also called a diskette and consists of _____

Floppy disks are widely used with personal computers _____

1. Formatting: preparing a floppy disk for use [p. 5.4]

Formatting prepares _____

A track _____

A cylinder _____

A sector _____

A track sector _____

A cluster _____

The file allocation table (FAT) _____

The file allocation table for Windows 95 is called virtual file allocation table (VFAT).

A write-protect window _____

2. Floppy disk storage capacity [p. 5.6]

Amount of data that can be stored on a floppy disk depends on two factors: _____

_____

Recording density is _____

This measurement is referred to as bits per second (bpi).

Multiple zone recording (MZR) _____

Measurement of the number of tracks is referred to as tracks per inch (tpi).

High-density (HD) floppy disks _____

3. Storing data on a floppy disk [p. 5.6]

Data is stored on tracks of the disk using the same binary code that is used to store data in memory, such as ASCII.

A recording mechanism _____

_____

Access time is _____

Access time depends on:

_____ – _____

_____ – _____

_____ – _____

4. The care of floppy disks [p. 5.8]

When handling floppy disks _____

_____
_____
_____

B. Hard disks [p. 5.8]

Consist of _____

_____

Minicomputers and mainframes use hard disks called fixed disks or direct-access storage devices (DASD).

1. Hard disk storage capacity [p. 5.9]

Hard disks contain one or more disk platters, and each platter surface can be used to store data.

Before a hard disk is formatted, it can be divided into partitions, which are _____

_____

On personal computers, partitions are _____

Storage capacity is measured in _____, _____, or

_____

2. Storing data on a hard disk [p. 5.10]

Similar to storing data on floppy disks

Hard disk read/write heads are attached to access arms that _____

_____

A head crash is _____

Access time is faster for a hard disk than for a floppy disk for two reasons:

_____
_____

Some computers improve the apparent speed at which data is written to and read from a disk by using disk cache, which is _____

_____

Controllers are electronic circuits that manage the flow of data to and from the hard disk.

Two common types of controllers on PCs:

Integrated drive electronics (IDE) controllers _____

_____

Small computer system interface (SCSI) controllers _____

_____

C. Disk cartridges [p. 5.11]

Disk cartridges, a variation of disk storage available for use with PCs, _____

_____

The Bernoulli disk cartridge _____

_____

D. Maintaining data stored on a disk [p. 5.12]

Two procedures should be performed on a regular basis to prevent loss of disk data:

1. Backup [p. 5.12]

(continued)

Backup is _____

_____

2. Defragmentation [p. 5.12]

A disk drive is fragmented when _____

_____

Defragmentation _____

_____

3. Data compression [p. 5.13]

Reduces storage requirements by _____

Types of compression:

Lossless compression is _____

Lossy compression is _____

III. CD-ROM and optical disks [p. 5.14]

Large quantities of data can be stored on optical disks, which use laser technology to read from and write data to a plastic disk or platter.

Data is written on an optical disk _____

_____

Up to 150 14-inch optical disks can be installed in automated disk library systems called jukeboxes that provide more than one trillion bytes of storage.

CD-ROM is an acronym for _____

A CD-ROM can store _____

A CD-ROM called DVD (digital video disk) _____

A CD-ROM drive's speed rating refers to how fast the drive can transfer data in relation to a standard established for CD-ROM drives used for multimedia applications.

Recordable CD-ROM drives are called _____

Erasable CD-ROM drives are called _____

Magneto-optical technology, used by the most common erasable optical drives, changes the polarity of a spot on the disk that has been heated by a laser.

A floptical disk is _____

IV. Magnetic tape [p. 5.16]

During the 1950s and 1960s was primary method of storing data

Serves as the primary means _____

_____

Consists of _____

Tape is considered a sequential storage media because _____

_____

A. Cartridge tape devices [p. 5.16]

A cartridge tape contains _____

1/4-inch cartridge tapes, mounted internally or externally, used for backup on PCs

1/2-inch cartridge tapes, usually mounted in their own cabinet, used for larger systems

B. Reel-to-reel tape devices [p. 5.17]

Use two reels: _____

_____

C. Storing data on magnetic tape [p. 5.18]

Binary codes, such as ASCII and EBCDIC, are used to represent data

Several different methods used to record bits on the tape

Quarter-inch-cartridge (QIC) tape devices _____

_____

Longitudinal or serpentine recording method works by _____

_____

Digital audio tape (DAT) drives use helical scan technology to _____

_____

Tape density is _____

V. Other types of storage devices [p. 5.19]

A. PC Cards [p. 5.19]

PC Cards are _____

_____

Most often used with portable computers

B. RAID storage systems [p. 5.19]

RAID (redundant array of inexpensive disks) is _____

_____

RAID level 1 is sometimes called disk mirroring because _____

_____

Striping, used in RAID levels beyond level 1, divides _____

_____

Advantages offered by RAID over single large expensive disks (SLEDs): ____

_____

C. Mass storage systems [p. 5.21]

Provide _____

Ideal for large databases that require all information to be readily accessible

Mass storage systems can retrieve _____

_____

D. Special-purpose storage devices [p. 5.21]

Memory buttons are _____

_____

Smart cards are _____

_____

(continued)

Optical memory cards can _____

_____

VI.   Summary of storage [p. 5.23]

Storage is used _____

_____

TERMS

access arms [p. 5.10]
access time [p. 5.7]
auxiliary storage [p. 5.2]

backup [p. 5.12]
Bernoulli disk cartridge
   [p. 5.11]
bits per inch (bpi) [p. 5.6]

cartridge tape [p. 5.16]
CD-E (compact disk-erasable)
   [p. 5.15]
CD-R (compact disk-recordable)
   [p. 5.15]
CD-ROM [p. 5.14]
cluster [p. 5.4]
compact disk read-only memory
   [p. 5.14]
cylinder [p. 5.4]

data compression [p. 5.13]
data transfer rate [p. 5.7]
defragmentation [p. 5.12]
digital audio tape (DAT)
   [p. 5.18]
direct-access storage devices
   (DASD) [p. 5.9]
disk cache [p. 5.10]
disk cartridges [p. 5.11]
disk mirroring [p. 5.20]
diskette [p. 5.3]
DVD (digital video disk)
   [p. 5.14]

file allocation table (FAT)
   [p. 5.5]
fixed disks [p. 5.9]

floppy disk [p. 5.3]
floptical [p. 5.15]
formatting [p. 5.4]
fragmented [p. 5.12]

hard disks [p. 5.8]
hard disk controller [p. 5.10]
head crash [p. 5.10]
helical scan technology
   [p. 5.18]
hierarchical storage management
   (HSM) [p. 5.24]
high-density (HD) floppy disk
   [p. 5.6]

integrated drive electronics (IDE)
   [p. 5.11]

latency [p. 5.7]
longitudinal recording [p. 5.18]

magnetic disk [p. 5.3]
magnetic tape [p. 5.16]
magneto-optical (MO) [p. 5.15]
mass storage [p. 5.21]
memory buttons [p. 5.21]
multiple zone recording
   (MZR) [p. 5.6]

near-line storage [p. 5.24]
nonvolatile [p. 5.2]

offline storage [p. 5.24]
online storage [p. 5.24]
optical disks [p. 5.14]
optical memory cards
   [p. 5.22]

partitions [p. 5.9]
PC Cards [p. 5.19]

platters [p. 5.8]
Quarter-Inch-Cartridge (QIC)
   [p. 5.18]
RAID [p. 5.19]
read/write head [p. 5.7]
reading data [p. 5.2]
recording data [p. 5.2]
recording density [p. 5.6]
redundant array of inexpensive
   disks [p. 5.19]
reel-to-reel tape [p. 5.17]
rotational delay [p. 5.7]

secondary storage [p. 5.2]
sector [p. 5.4]
seek time [p. 5.7]
sequential storage [p. 5.16]
serpentine recording [p. 5.18]
SLEDs [p. 5.20]
small computer system interface
   (SCSI) [p. 5.11]
smart cards [p. 5.22]
storage [p. 5.2]
striping [p. 5.20]

tape density [p. 5.18]
track [p. 5.4]
track sector [p. 5.4]
tracks per inch (tpi) [p. 5.6]

virtual file allocation table
   (VFAT) [p. 5.5]
volatile [p. 5.2]

write-protect window [p. 5.5]
writing data [p. 5.2]

SELF TEST
True/False

_____ 1. Storage is volatile, which means when the power is turned off, data and programs are erased.

_____ 2. The formatting process analyzes the recording surface for defective spots.

_____ 3. The number of tracks and sectors created on a floppy disk when it is formatted varies based on the capacity of the floppy disk, the capabilities of the floppy disk drive being used, and the specifications of the operating system software that does the formatting.

_____ 4. The amount of data you can store on a floppy disk depends on two factors: the recording density and the number of tracks on the floppy disk.

_____ 5. The time required to locate the data on the storage device and transfer it to memory is called seek time.

_____ 6. Hard disk read/write heads, which are attached to access arms, actually touch the surface of the disk.

_____ 7. SCSI devices connect to each other in a chain, which is a cable between each device.

_____ 8. The lossy compression technique substitutes codes for repeating patterns.

_____ 9. Digital audio tape (DAT) uses helical scan technology to record data across the width of the tape at a six-degree angle.

_____ 10. Because multiple read or write operations must take place at the same time, data cannot be read from or written to RAID disks as fast as with single large expensive disks (SLEDs).

Matching

1. _____ floppy disk
2. _____ file allocation table (FAT)
3. _____ read/write head
4. _____ hard disk
5. _____ head crash
6. _____ disk cache
7. _____ disk cartridge
8. _____ quarter-inch-cartridge (QIC)
9. _____ PC Cards
10. _____ RAID storage systems

a. read/write head colliding and damaging the hard disk surface, causing a loss of data

b. offers the storage and fast access features of hard disks and the portability of floppy disks

c. uses the latest in RAM technology to provide high-speed data access and retrieval

d. stores the file name, file size, when the file was last changed, and the cluster number where the file begins

e. small, credit card-sized card that fit into PC Card expansion slots

f. creating a copy of important programs and data to prevent loss of disk data

g. circuit board that has a hard disk built onto it, providing an easy way to expand storage capacity

h. circular piece of thin mylar plastic that is coated with an oxide material

i. group of integrated small disks that acts like a single large disk drive

j. contains magnetic recording tape in a small, rectangular, plastic housing

k. rests on the top and bottom surface of a rotating floppy disk, generating electronic impulses

l. stores enormous quantities of information by using a laser to burn holes on the disk surface

m. area of memory set aside for data most often read from the disk

n. records the data in narrow tracks along the length of the tape

o. rigid platters coated with a material that allows data to be magnetically recorded

Multiple Choice

_____   1. Where are programs and data stored when they are *not* being processed?
   a.   memory
   b.   primary storage
   c.   RAM (random access memory)
   d.   storage (secondary or auxiliary)

_____   2. Which of the following is *not* part of the formatting process?
   a.   define tracks
   b.   partition the disk
   c.   erase data
   d.   analyze the recording surface

_____   3. What is the mechanism used to protect data from being erased accidentally during formatting or other writing operations?
   a.   file allocation table
   b.   a special command in format
   c.   write-protect window
   d.   multiple zone recording

_____   4. What is a cluster?
   a.   a narrow recording band forming a full circle around a diskette
   b.   all tracks of the same number
   c.   a pie-shaped section of a floppy disk
   d.   the smallest unit of floppy disk space used to store data

_____   5. What is rotational delay?
   a.   the time required to transfer data from storage to memory
   b.   the time it takes for the sector containing data to rotate under the read/write head
   c.   the time required to locate and transfer data from storage to memory
   d.   the time it takes to position the read/write head over the proper track

_____   6. Why is access time for a hard disk significantly faster than for a floppy disk?
   a.   hard disk read/write heads actually touch the surface of the disk
   b.   a hard disk spins ten to twenty times faster and is always spinning
   c.   only one surface of a hard disk platter can be used to store data
   d.   most personal computers can support more than 100 high-speed hard disk drives

_____   7. What is data compression?
   a.   reducing the storage requirements of data by substituting codes for repeating patterns
   b.   preparing a floppy disk so it can store data by defining the tracks, cylinders, and sectors
   c.   dividing a logical piece of data into smaller parts and writing the parts on multiple drives
   d.   reorganizing the data stored on disk so files are located in contiguous clusters

_____   8. Sixteen-speed CD-ROM drives can transfer how many kilobytes per second (kbps)?
   a.   150 kbps
   b.   1,500 kbps
   c.   1,800 kbps
   d.   2,400 kbps

_____   9. For what purpose is magnetic tape no longer used?
   a.   as a cost-effective way to store data that does not have to be accessed immediately
   b.   as a means of backup for most medium and large computer systems
   c.   as the primary method of storage on personal computers
   d.   as a way of transferring data from one large computer system to another

_____ 10. What is an optical memory card?
    a. a special-purpose storage device about the size of a dime that can currently hold about 8,000 characters of information
    b. a special-purpose storage device the size and thickness of a credit card that contains a microprocessor capable of storing recorded information
    c. a special-purpose storage device that can store up to 4.1 MB of digitized text or images on a device the size of a credit card
    d. a storage device that provides automated retrieval of data from a library of storage media such as tape or data cartridges

Fill in the Blanks

1. _____ devices provide a more permanent form of storage than memory because they are nonvolatile, that is, data and programs are retained when power is turned off.

2. The original floppy disks introduced by IBM were called _____, a term that is still used, because they were thin and flexible.

3. A(n) _____ is a narrow recording band forming a full circle around the floppy disk.

4. In addition to defining the floppy disk recording surface, the _____ process erases any data that is on the floppy disk, analyzes the floppy disk recording surface for any defective spots, and establishes a directory that will be used to record information about files on the floppy disk.

5. _____ controllers, which are common on personal computers, can operate one or two hard disk drives and transfer data to the disk at a rate of up to 10 MB per second.

6. The term _____ is used to describe a file stored in clusters that are not next to each other, or the condition of a disk drive that has many files stored in noncontiguous clusters.

7. Tape is considered a(n) _____ media because the computer must write and read tape records one after another.

8. _____ is the number of bits that can be stored on one inch of magnetic tape.

9. Dividing a logical piece of data such as a record or word into smaller parts and writing those parts on multiple drives is called _____.

10. _____, which are small storage devices about the size of a dime and look like watch batteries, are used in applications where information about an item must travel with the item.

Complete the Table

TYPE	SPACE WITH CAPACITY	DESCRIPTION
Magnetic Disk		Thin, portable plastic storage media that is reliable and low cost.
Floppy disk	_____	
Hard disk	500 MB to 5 GB	
_____	_____	Removable hard disk unit that provides large storage capacity and is portable.
CD-ROM and Optical Disk	_____	High-capacity disks use lasers to read and record data.
Magnetic Tape	120 MB to 4 GB	
_____		
Reel tape	_____	1/2-inch tape on 300- to 3,600-foot reel.
Other Storage Devices PC Card	_____	Credit card-sized disk used on portable computers.
_____	5 GB to 40 GB	
_____	10 TB to 100 TB	Automated retrieval of storage media such as tape cartridges.
Special-Purpose Devices _____	8 KB	
Smart card	_____	Thin microprocessor embedded in plastic card
_____	4 GB	_____

Things to Think About

1. How is primary storage different from storage?

2. Why is magnetic disk a direct-access storage device (DASD), while magnetic tape is a sequential storage device?

3. How does RAID technology reduce the risk of losing data?

4. Why might optical disks someday replace data now stored on film such as microfiche?

Puzzle

Word search. All the words described below appear in the puzzle. Words may be either forward, backward, across, up, down, or diagonal. Circle each word as you find it.

L	O	S	S	L	E	S	S	💻	S	M	A	R	T
I	R	O	N	💾	D	T	E	S	M	Z	A	B	A
E	Z	📁	I	C	E	R	E	P	A	R	A	E	F
G	N	M	C	S	I	A	K	A	R	K	O	R	C
D	R	O	S	A	I	L	T	R	A	C	X	N	P
I	F	R	A	I	D	💾	I	T	D	A	P	O	C
R	O	D	E	T	N	E	M	G	A	R	F	U	A
T	💻	C	A	M	E	D	E	D	E	T	R	L	D
R	G	I	G	A	B	Y	T	E	H	📁	A	L	S
A	B	D	E	E	T	I	N	R	A	N	B	I	P
C	I	E	I	H	💾	N	A	C	S	I	L	E	H
G	N	I	P	P	I	R	T	S	C	S	I	H	💻
📁	C	A	B	A	C	K	U	P	C	C	A	R	D

unique type of disk cartridge works with a special drive unit that uses a cushion of air

tape that contains the magnetic recording tape in a small, rectangular, plastic housing

creating a copy of important programs and data

directory created with DOS operating system used to record information about files

dividing a logical piece of data into smaller parts and writing them on multiple drives

technology that writes data at higher densities across tape at an angle

unit used to measure recording density

controllers that can operate one or two hard drives

controllers that can support up to seven disk drives or any mix of up to seven devices

a billion bytes

crash that results when hard disk read/write head collides with and damages disk surface

group of integrated small disks that acts like a single large disk drive

cards that fit into PCMCIA expansion slots, most often used on portable computers

small optical disks that use the same laser technology used for recording music

cards that contain a thin microprocessor capable of storing recorded information

narrow recording band forming a full circle around a floppy disk

method that records data at the same density on all floppy disk tracks

the time it takes to position the read/write head over the proper track

type of compression where no data is lost in the process

when a file is stored in clusters that are not next to each other

SELF TEST ANSWERS

True/False

1. *F* [p. 5.2]
2. *T* [p. 5.5]
3. *T* [p. 5.5]
4. *T* [p. 5.6]
5. *F* [p. 5.7]
6. *F* [p. 5.10]
7. *T* [p. 5.11]
8. *F* [p. 5.13]
9. *T* [p. 5.18]
10. *F* [p. 5.20]

Matching

1. *h* [p. 5.3]
2. *d* [p. 5.5]
3. *k* [p. 5.7]
4. *o* [p. 5.8]
5. *a* [p. 5.10]
6. *m* [p. 5.10]
7. *b* [p. 5.11]
8. *n* [p. 5.18]
9. *e* [p. 5.19]
10. *i* [p. 5.19]

Multiple Choice

1. *d* [p. 5.2]
2. *b* [p. 5.5]
3. *c* [p. 5.5]
4. *d* [p. 5.5]
5. *b* [p. 5.7]
6. *b* [p. 5.10]
7. *a* [p. 5.13]
8. *d* [p. 5.15]
9. *c* [p. 5.16]
10. *c* [p. 5.22]

Fill in the Blanks

1. *Storage* [p. 5.2]
2. *floppy disks or floppies* [p. 5.3]
3. *tracks* [p. 5.4]
4. *formatting* [p. 5.5]
5. *Integrated drive electronics (IDE)* [p. 5.11]
6. *fragmented* [p. 5.12]
7. *sequential storage* [p. 5.16]
8. *Tape density* [p. 5.18]
9. *striping* [p. 5.20]
10. *Memory buttons* [p. 5.21]

Complete the Table [p. 5.23]

TYPE		SPACE WITH CAPACITY	DESCRIPTION
Magnetic Disk			Thin, portable plastic storage media that is reliable and low cost.
	Floppy disk	*1.44 MB*	
	Hard disk	500 MB to 5 GB	*Fixed-platter storage media that provides large storage capacity and fast access.*
	Disk cartridge	*100 MB to 1 GB*	Removable hard disk unit that provides large storage capacity and is portable.
CD-ROM and Optical Disk		*650 MB to 7 GB*	High-capacity disks use lasers to read and record data.
Magnetic Tape			*Tape enclosed in rectangular plastic housing.*
	Cartridge tape	120 MB to 4 GB	
	Reel tape	*200 MB*	1/2-inch tape on 300- to 3,600-foot reel.
Other Storage Devices	PC Card	*40 MB to 300 MB*	Credit card-sized disk used on portable computers.
	RAID	5 GB to 40 GB	*Multiple hard disks integrated into a single unit.*
	Mass storage	10 TB to 100 TB	Automated retrieval of storage media such as tape cartridges.
Special-Purpose Devices	*Memory button*	8 KB	*Stores data on chip in small metal canister.*
	Smart card	*1 KB to 8 KB*	Thin microprocessor embedded in plastic card.
	Optical memory card	4 GB	*Text and images stored in credit card-sized holder.*

Puzzle Answer

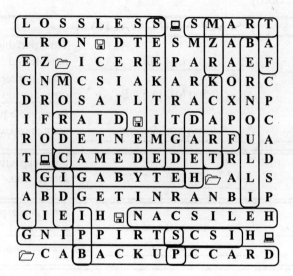

CHAPTER 6
Communications and Networks

CHAPTER OVERVIEW

This chapter begins by defining communications with an emphasis on the use of computers. The chapter immediately discusses twelve examples of how communications technology is used. Next, a communications system model is described. You discover various transmission media, line configurations, and characteristics of communications channels. Communications software and equipment are explained. The various types of communications networks are explained, followed by a discussion about communications network configurations. Here you learn how networks are joined and the importance of communications protocols. Finally, you are presented with an example of a communications network.

CHAPTER OBJECTIVES

After completing this chapter, you will be able to:

* Define the term communications

* Describe several uses of communications technology

* Describe the basic components of a communications system

* Describe the various transmission media used for communications channels

* Describe the different types of line configurations

* Describe how data is transmitted

* Describe the functions performed by communications software

* Describe commonly used communications equipment

* Explain the difference between local and wide area networks

* Explain the use of communications protocols

CHAPTER OUTLINE

I. What is communications? [p. 6.2]

   Sometimes called data communications or telecommunications

   Refers to _____

   _____

(continued)

II. Examples of how communications is used [p. 6.2]

The ability to instantly and accurately communicate information is changing the way people do business and interact with each other.

A. Electronic mail (e-mail) [p. 6.2]

Allows you _____

The other users _____

B. Voice mail [p. 6.2]

_____

_____

C. Facsimile (fax) [p. 6.2]

_____

_____

D. Telecommuting [p. 6.2]

_____

_____

E. Videoconferencing [p. 6.3]

_____

_____

F. Groupware [p. 6.4]

Software that helps _____

Is part of a broad concept _____

Features and capabilities include _____, _____,

_____, _____, and _____

G. Electronic data interchange (EDI) [p. 6.4]

_____

_____

Advantages of EDI over paper documents: _____

_____

_____

H. Global positioning systems (GPSs) [p. 6.5]

_____

_____

I. Bulletin board systems (BBSs) [p. 6.5]

_____

_____

BBSs are run by _____

J. Online services [p. 6.6]

_____

_____

K. The Internet [p. 6.7]

Is a _____

_____

III. A communications system model [p. 6.8]

Equipment in a basic model for a communications system:

* _____

* _____

* _____

* _____

* _____

The basic model also includes communications software that manage _____

_____

A communications channel is the path _____

Also called _____, _____, or _____

IV. Transmission media [p. 6.9]

Transmission media are _____

Two types – those that use physical cabling and those that use wireless technology

A. Twisted-pair cable [p. 6.9]

Consists of _____

Shielded twisted-pair (STP) cable _____

Unshielded twisted-pair (UTP) cable also is called _____

_____

B. Coaxial cable [p. 6.9]

Often referred to as coax, it is _____

_____

_____

One type of coaxial cable is used for cable television.

The other type is called _____

_____

C. Fiber-optic cable [p. 6.10]

Fiber-optic cable uses _____

The major advantages of fiber-optic cable _____

_____

Another advantage _____

Fiber-optic cable costs more than twisted-pair or coaxial cable and can be difficult to install and modify.

D. Microwave transmission [p. 6.11]

Microwaves are _____

Earth-based microwave transmission, called _____

(continued)

Microwaves are limited to line-of-sight transmission, which means _____

_____

Communications satellites _____

_____

Earth stations use _____

Transmission *to* the satellite is an uplink, and transmission *from* the satellite is a downlink.

Communications satellites usually are placed about 22,300 miles above earth in a geosynchronous

orbit, meaning _____

Very small aperture terminal (VSAT) antenna _____

E. Wireless transmission: radio and light waves [p. 6.12]

Uses one of three techniques to transmit data: _____ , _____ ,

and _____

A cellular telephone uses _____

F. An example of a communications channel [p. 6.14]

Steps that would occur:

1. _____
2. _____
3. _____
4. _____
5. _____
6. _____
7. _____

V. Line configurations [p. 6.14]

Two major line configurations (types of line connections) – point-to-point lines, and multidrop, or multipoint, lines

A. Point-to-point lines [p. 6.14]

Direct line between sending and receiving device

1. Switched line [p. 6.14]

Uses _____

_____

The process of establishing _____

Advantages of switched line – _____

Disadvantage of switched line – _____

2. Dedicated line [p. 6.15]

A dedicated line is a line connection that always is established.

A leased line or private line is _____

B. Multidrop lines [p. 6.15]

Also called _____

Commonly used to _____

Number of terminals is a decision made by designer based on anticipated traffic

Almost always uses leased line, and can decrease line _____

_____

VI. Characteristics of communications channels [p. 6.16]

    A. Types of signals: digital and analog [p. 6.16]

        Digital signals are _____

        Analog signals are _____

        Digital data service – communications channels designed to carry digital signals

        A T1 digital line _____

        A T3 digital line _____

        ISDN (integrated services digital network) is _____

        _____

    B. Transmission modes: asynchronous and synchronous [p. 6.17]

        In asynchronous transmission mode, _____

        _____

        In synchronous transmission mode, _____

        _____

    C. Direction of transmission: simplex, half-duplex, and full-duplex [p. 6.18]

        In simplex transmission, _____

        In half-duplex transmission, _____

        In full-duplex transmission, _____

    D. Transmission rate [p. 6.18]

        Determined by a communications channel's bandwidth and speed.

        Bandwidth is _____

        The speed at which data _____

VII. Communications software [p. 6.19]

Some communications equipment is preprogrammed to accomplish its intended communications task.

Communications software manages _____

_____

Dialing feature _____

File transfer feature _____

Terminal emulation feature _____

Internet access feature _____

VIII. Communications equipment [p. 6.19]

    A. Modems [p. 6.19]

        A computer's digital signals _____

        A modem converts the digital signal of a computer to analog signals and converts the analog back to digital signals that can be used by the computer.

(continued)

The word modem comes from a combination of the words _____

_____

An external modem is _____

An internal modem is _____

B. Multiplexers [p. 6.20]

Sometimes referred to as an MUX, combines _____

A mulitplexer increases _____

C. Front-end processors [p. 6.21]

Computer dedicated to handling communications requirements of a larger computer

Tasks handled: _____, _____, and

_____.

D. _____ [p. 6.21]

Is a circuit card _____

E. Wiring hubs [p. 6.22]

A wiring hub (concentrator or multistation access unit (MAU)), allows _____

_____

Acts as the _____

Generally contains _____

A stackable hub is _____

F. Gateways [p. 6.22]

A gateway is _____

G. Bridges [p. 6.22]

A bridge is _____

H. Routers [p. 6.22]

Are used _____

A router is _____

_____

Routers can determine alternative routes in case of a partial network failure.

IX. Communications networks [p. 6.23]

Is a collection of _____

_____

A. Local area networks (LANs) [p. 6.23]

Communications network that covers a limited geographic area

1. LAN applications:

Hardware resource sharing _____

A server is a _____

Software resource sharing involves _____

Network licenses or site licenses allow _____

Information resource sharing allows _____

2. File-server and client-server networks [p. 6.24]

Using the file-server method, the server _____

With the client-server method, the server _____

Steps of file-server:

1. _____

2. _____

3. _____

4. _____

Steps of client-server:

1. _____

2. _____

3. _____

4. _____

A database server is _____

An application server is _____

3. Peer-to-peer networks [p. 6.25]

Allow _____

4. Network operating systems [p. 6.25]

Is _____

_____

Tasks of the network operating system (NOS) include:

• _____

• _____

• _____

• _____

Some examples of peer-to-peer network software are _____

_____

Novell's NetWare, Microsoft's Advanced NT Server, and IBM's LAN Server are examples of network operating systems.

B. _____ [p. 6.26]

Geographic in scope (as opposed to local); uses telephone cables, terrestrial microwave, satellites, or a variety of communications channels.

A metropolitan area network (MAN) is _____

Public WAN companies include common carriers such as telephone companies.

Value-added carriers _____

Value-added networks (VAN) enhance _____

Packet-switching _____

X. Network configurations [p. 6.27]

Topology is the configuration, or physical layout, of equipment in a communications network.

(continued)

Nodes are _____

Workstations are _____

    A.   Star network [p. 6.27]

        A star network has _____

        _____

    B.   Bus network [p. 6.28]

        In a bus network, _____

        _____

    C.   Ring network [p. 6.29]

        In a ring network, _____

        _____

XI. Communications protocols [p. 6.29]

    A protocol is _____

    _____

    Protocols define _____

    The two most widely used protocols for networks are _____ and

    _____

    A.   Ethernet [p. 6.30]

        Is the most widely used network protocol for LAN networks

        Is based on _____

        _____

        Because Ethernet uses a bus topology, packets of data can be sent in both directions

        A collision occurs _____

        Ethernet uses _____

        _____

    B.   Token ring [p. 6.31]

        Second most widely used protocol for LAN networks

        A token ring network _____

        _____

        Devices on the network that want to send a message _____

        The *ring* in token ring _____

        It does not mean _____

XII. An example of a communications network [p. 6.32]

    _____

    _____

    _____

    _____

XIII. Summary of communications and networks [p. 6.33]

    Communications technology continues to change _____

    _____

Enterprise computing is _____

TERMS

10base2 cable [p. 6.10]
10baseT cable [p. 6.9]

analog signal [p. 6.16]
application server [p. 6.25]
asynchronous transmission mode
    [p. 6.17]

bandwidth [p. 6.18]
bits per second (bps)
    [p. 6.18]
bridge [p. 6.22]
bulletin board system (BBS)
    [p. 6.5]
bus network [p. 6.28]

carrier sense multiple access
    with collision detection
    (CSMA/CD) [p. 6.30]
cellular telephone [p. 6.13]
client-server [p. 6.24]
coax [p. 6.9]
coaxial cable [p. 6.9]
collision [p. 6.30]
common carriers [p. 6.26]
communications [p. 6.2]
communications channel
    [p. 6.8]
communications line [p. 6.8]
communications link [p. 6.8]
communications satellites
    [p. 6.11]
communications software
    [p. 6.8, 6.19]
concentrator [p. 6.22]

data communications [p. 6.2]
data link [p. 6.8]
database server [p. 6.25]
dedicated line [p. 6.15]
dialing [p. 6.19]
digital data service [p. 6.17]
digital signal [p. 6.16]
downlink [p. 6.11]

earth stations [p. 6.11]
electronic data interchange (EDI)
    [p. 6.4]
electronic mail (e-mail) [p. 6.2]

enterprise computing [p. 6.33]
Ethernet [p. 6.30]
external modem [p. 6.19]

facsimile [p. 6.2]
Fast-Ethernet [p. 6.30]
fax [p. 6.2]
fiber-optic cable [p. 6.10]
file-server [p. 6.24]
file transfer [p. 6.19]
front-end processor [p. 6.21]
full-duplex transmission
    [p. 6.18]

gateway [p. 6.22]
geosynchronous orbit
    [p. 6.12]
global positioning system (GPS)
    [p. 6.5]
groupware [p. 6.4]

half-duplex transmission
    [p. 6.18]
handshake [p. 6.14]
hardware resource sharing
    [p. 6.23]
host computer [p. 6.15]

information resource sharing
    [p. 6.24]
information services [p. 6.6]
internal modem [p. 6.20]
Internet [p. 6.7]
Internet access [p. 6.19]
intranets [p. 6.7]
ISDN (integrated services digital
    network) [p. 6.17]

leased line [p. 6.15]
line configurations [p. 6.14]
local area network (LAN)
    [p. 6.23]

metropolitan area network (MAN)
    [p. 6.26]
microwaves [p. 6.11]
modem [p. 6.19]
multidrop line [p. 6.15]
multiplexer [p. 6.20]
multipoint line [p. 6.15]

multistation access unit (MAU)
    [p. 6.22]

network [p. 6.23]
network interface card (NIC)
    [p. 6.21]
network licenses [p. 6.24]
network operating system (NOS)
    [p. 6.25]
node [p. 6.27]

online services [p. 6.6]

packet-switching [p. 6.26]
peer-to-peer network
    [p. 6.25]
point-to-point line [p. 6.14]
polling [p. 6.21]
private line [p. 6.15]
protocol [p. 6.29]

ring network [p. 6.29]
router [p. 6.22]

shielded twisted-pair (STP)
    cable [p. 6.9]
simplex transmission [p. 6.18]
site licenses [p. 6.24]
software resource sharing
    [p. 6.24]
stackable hub [p. 6.22]
star network [p. 6.27]
switched line [p. 6.14]
synchronous transmission mode
    [p. 6.18]
sys op [p. 6.5]
system operator [p. 6.5]

T1 [p. 6.17]
T3 [p. 6.17]
telecommunications [p. 6.2]
telecommuting [p. 6.2]
terminal emulation [p. 6.19]
terrestrial microwave [p. 6.11]
thinnet [p. 6.10]
token [p. 6.31]
token ring network [p. 6.31]
transmission media [p. 6.9]
twisted-pair cable [p. 6.9]
                    (continued)

unshielded twisted-pair (UTP)
  cable [p. 6.9]
uplink [p. 6.11]
value-added carriers [p. 6.26]
value-added network (VAN)
  [p. 6.26]

very small aperture terminal
  (VSAT) [p. 6.12]
video conferencing [p. 6.3]
voice mail [p. 6.2]

wide area network (WAN)
  [p. 6.26]

wireless transmission
  [p. 6.12]
wiring hub [p. 6.22]
workgroup technology
  [p. 6.4]
workstations [p. 6.27]

SELF TEST
True/False

_____ 1. Telecommuting involves working at home and communicating with an office by using a personal computer and communications equipment and software.

_____ 2. The basic model of a communications system includes communications software.

_____ 3. The microwave transmission *to* the satellite is called a downlink.

_____ 4. An advantage of using a dedicated line is that a connection always is established, unlike a switched line connection, which must be reestablished each time it is used.

_____ 5. In asynchronous transmission mode, large blocks of data are transmitted at regular intervals, eliminating the need for start and stop bits for each byte.

_____ 6. A modem is necessary only at the sending end of a communications channel.

_____ 7. A bridge could be used to connect a local area network of personal computers to a mainframe computer network.

_____ 8. The file-server method of information resource sharing greatly reduces the amount of data sent over a network but requires a more powerful server system than the client-server method.

_____ 9. A star network often is used when the central computer contains all the data required to process the input from terminals, such as an airline reservation system.

_____ 10. Using the same protocols, different types and makes of computers can communicate with each other.

Matching

1. _____ electronic mail
2. _____ voice mail
3. _____ fax equipment
4. _____ telecommuting
5. _____ videoconferencing
6. _____ groupware
7. _____ electronic data interchange (EDI)
8. _____ global positioning system (GPS)
9. _____ bulletin board system (BBS)
10. _____ online service

a. used to transmit a digitized image of a document over telephone lines

b. capability of individuals to work at home and communicate with their offices using PCs

c. for a fee, provides information and services to users who subscribe

d. uses satellites to determine the geographic location of earth-based equipment

e. allows a personal computer to imitate or appear to be a specific type of terminal

f. converts data at the sending end into an unrecognizable string of characters

g. capability to use computers to transmit messages to and receive messages from other users

h. combination of hardware and software used to connect similar networks

i.   capability to electronically exchange documents from one business's computer system to another

j.   maintains a centralized collection of information in the form of electronic messages

k.   software that helps multiple users to collaborate on projects and share information

l.   converts the digital signals of a terminal or computer to analog signals that are transmitted

m.   uses computers, television cameras, communications software and equipment to conduct electronic meetings

n.   combines more than one input signal into a single stream of data that can be transmitted

o.   digitizes messages so the messages can be stored on disk like other computer data

Multiple Choice

_____ 1. What term refers to the transmission of data and information between two or more computers, using a communications channel such as a telephone line?
  a.   telecommunications
  b.   teleprocessing
  c.   teleconferencing
  d.   telecommuting

_____ 2. Which of the following is *not* essential equipment in the basic model of a communications system?
  a.   computer output microfilm
  b.   computer or terminal
  c.   communications equipment
  d.   communications channel

_____ 3. What is the advantage of using twisted-pair cable as a transmission medium?
  a.   it is unaffected by outside electrical interference
  b.   it can transmit data at higher data rates over longer distances than coaxial cable
  c.   it offers substantial weight and time savings and increased speed of transmission
  d.   it is inexpensive and can be installed easily

_____ 4. What are two major line configurations commonly used in communications?
  a.   physical cabling lines and wireless lines
  b.   file-server lines and client-server lines
  c.   point-to-point lines and multidrop lines
  d.   synchronous lines and asynchronous lines

_____ 5. A citizens band radio, on which a user either can talk or listen but cannot do both at the same time, is an example of what type of transmission?
  a.   simplex
  b.   multiplex
  c.   half-duplex
  d.   full-duplex

(continued)

_____ 6. What does a modem do?

    a. converts the digital signals of a computer to analog signals that are transmitted over a communications channel

    b. combines more than one input signal into a single stream of data that can be transmitted over a communications channel

    c. handles the communications requirements of a larger computer and communicates the processed data

    d. attaches to the cable or wireless technology used to connect devices in a network and coordinates the transmission, receipt, and error checking of data

_____ 7. What communications software feature allows a personal computer to imitate or appear to be a specific type of input device so the personal computer can connect to another, usually larger, computer?

    a. dialing

    b. file transfer

    c. terminal emulation

    d. data encryption

_____ 8. A company has local area networks of personal computers in both its accounting and marketing departments. What could be used to connect the two networks?

    a. a gateway

    b. a bridge

    c. a router

    d. a portal

_____ 9. Hardware, software, and information resource sharing are three common applications of what type of network?

    a. local area network (LAN)

    b. wide area network (WAN)

    c. metropolitan area network (MAN)

    d. value-added network (VAN)

_____ 10. What is a bus network?

    a. a network that contains a central computer and one or more terminals or personal computers connected to it

    b. a network with all the devices connected to and sharing a single data path, transmitting information in both directions

    c. a network with a circle of computers communicating with one another, without a host computer, transmitting data in one direction only

    d. a network that constantly circulates an electronic signal that must be taken and attached to a message before it is sent

Fill in the Blanks

1. Groupware is part of a broad concept called _____, which includes equipment and software that help group members communicate and manage their activities.

2. The basic communications model also includes _____, consisting of programs that manage transmission of data between computers.

3. A(n) _____ is a high-quality communications line not susceptible to electrical interference and able to transmit data faster over longer distances.

4. _____ are radio waves that can be used to provide high-speed, line-of-sight transmission of both voice and data.

5. A(n) _____, which is a direct line between a sending and receiving device, may be one of two types: a switched line or a dedicated line.

6. Computer equipment is designed to process data as _____, which are individual electrical pulses that represent the bits grouped together in bytes.

7. A(n) _____ combines more than one input signal into a single stream of data that can be transmitted over a communications channel, which increases communications efficiency and reduces the cost of individual communications channels.

8. A(n) _____ is a computer dedicated to handling the communications requirements of a larger computer.

9. A(n) _____ is an intelligent network connecting device that sends communications traffic directly to the appropriate network.

10. Peer-to-peer networks are appropriate for a(n) _____ of users who work primarily on their own computers and need only to use the resources of other computers occasionally.

Complete the Table

PROTOCOL	DESCRIPTION
Ethernet	_____
_____	Uses electronic token to avoid transmission conflict by allowing only one device to transmit at a time.
PowerTalk	_____
_____	Fiber Distributed Data Interface. High-speed fiber-optic protocol.
TCP/IP	_____
_____	Asynchronous Transmission Mode. Protocol developed for transmitting voice, data, and video over any type of media.
IPX	_____
_____	PC protocol that uses 1,024 byte blocks.
Zmodem	_____
_____	PC protocol that uses variable length blocks.

Things to Think About

1. Why would electronic data interchange (EDI) offer lower transaction costs, reduced time to transmit documents, reduced entry errors, and reduced paper flow when compared to paper documents?

2. Why is full-duplex transmission used for most interactive computer applications and for computer-to-computer data transmission?

3. Why are modems not needed with digital data service?

4. Why, in actual practice, are hardware resource sharing and information resource sharing often combined?

Puzzle

The terms described by each phrase below are written in code. Break the code by writing the correct term above the coded word. Then, use your broken code to translate the final sentence.

1. wire commonly used for telephone lines and to connect PCs

   twisted pair

   τωιστεδ παιρ

2. small diameter coax cable used for computer networks

   τηιννετ

3. the transmission from a satellite to a receiving earth station

   δοωνλινκ

4. abbreviation for antenna measuring only one to three meters in size

   ϖσατ

5. orbit in which the satellite rotates with the earth

   γεοσψνχηρονουσ

6. transmission that uses light beams, radio waves, or carrier-connect radio to transmit data

   ωιρελεσσ

7. type of telephone that uses radio waves to communicate with a local antenna assigned to a specific area

   χελλυλαρ

8. a direct line between a sending and receiving device

   ποιντ–το–ποιντ

9. process of establishing the communications connection with a switched line

   ηανδσηακε

10. type of line configuration commonly used to connect multiple devices on a single line to a main computer

    μυλτιποιντ

11. type of signal that comprises voice transmission

    αναλογ

12. type of transmission in which data can be sent in both directions at the same time

    φυλλ–δυπλεξ

13. range of frequencies that a communications channel can carry

    βανδωιδτη

14. type of processor that is a computer dedicated to handling communications requirements of a larger system

    φροντ–ενδ

15. checking connected terminals to see if they have data to send

    πολλινγ

16. allows commercial software to be accessed by many users

    σιτε λιχενσε

17. configuration of the equipment in a communications network   τοπολογψ

18. devices connected to a network   νοδεσ

19. type of network that contains a central computer and one or more PCs or terminals connected to it   σταρ

20. a set of rules and procedures for exchanging information between computers   προτοχολ

τηε βεστ πχ μοδεμσ ανδ φιβερ – οπτιχ χαβλεσ χαν τρανσμιτ

τηιρτψ – τηουσανδ σινγλε–σπαχεδ, τψπεωριττεν παγεσ ιν ονε

σεχονδ □ λιτεραλλψ φαστερ τηαν α σπεεδινγ βυλλετ.

SELF TEST ANSWERS

True/False
1. T [p. 6.2]
2. T [p. 6.8]
3. F [p. 6.11]
4. T [p. 6.15]
5. F [p. 6.17]
6. F [p. 6.19]
7. F [p. 6.22]
8. F [p. 6.24]
9. T [p. 6.27]
10. T [p. 6.29]

Matching
1. g [p. 6.2]
2. o [p. 6.2]
3. a [p. 6.2]
4. b [p. 6.2]
5. m [p. 6.3]
6. k [p. 6.4]
7. i [p. 6.4]
8. d [p. 6.5]
9. j [p. 6.5]
10. c [p. 6.6]

Multiple Choice
1. a [p. 6.2]
2. a [p. 6.8]
3. d [p. 6.9]
4. c [p. 6.14]
5. c [p. 6.18]
6. a [p. 6.19]
7. c [p. 6.19]
8. b [p. 6.22]
9. a [p. 6.23]
10. b [p. 6.28]

ill in the Blanks

1. *workgroup technology* [p. 6.4]
2. *communications software* [p. 6.8]
3. *coaxial cable* [p. 6.9]
4. *Microwaves* [p. 6.11]
5. *point-to-point line* [p. 6.14]

(continued)

6. *digital signals* [p. 6.16]

7. *multiplexer* or *MUX* [p. 6.20]

8. *front-end processor* [p. 6.21]

9. *router* [p. 6.22]

10. *small number* [p. 6.25]

Complete the Table [p. 6.29]

PROTOCOL	DESCRIPTION
Ethernet	*Most widely used protocol for LANs.*
Token ring	Uses electronic token to avoid transmission conflict by allowing only one device to transmit at a time.
PowerTalk	*Links Apple Macintosh computers.*
FDDI	Fiber Distributed Data Interface. High-speed fiber-optic protocol.
TCP/IP	*Transmission Control Protocol/Internet. Used on the Internet.*
ATM	Asynchronous Transmission Mode. Protocol developed for transmitting voice, data, and video over any type of media.
IPX	*Used on Novell NetWare networks.*
Ymodem	PC protocol that uses 1,024 byte blocks.
Zmodem	*PC protocol that uses 512 byte blocks.*
Kermit	PC protocol that uses variable length blocks.

Puzzle Answer

1. wire commonly used for telephone lines and to connect PCs

    twisted pair

    τωιστεδ παιρ

2. small diameter coax cable used for computer networks

    thinnet

    τηιννε

3. the transmission from a satellite to a receiving earth station

    downlink

    δοωνλινκ

4. abbreviation for antenna measuring only one to three meters in size

    VSAT

    ϖσατ

5. orbit in which the satellite rotates with the earth

    geosynchronous

    γεοσψνχηρονουσ

6. transmission that uses light beams, radio waves, or carrier-connect radio to transmit data

wireless
ωιρελεσσ

7. type of telephone that uses radio waves to communicate with a local antenna assigned to a specific area

cellular
χελλυλαρ

8. a direct line between a sending and receiving device

point-to-point
ποιντ–το–ποιντ

9. process of establishing the communications connection with a switched line

handshake
ηανδσηακε

10. type of line configuration commonly used to connect multiple devices on a single line to a main computer

multipoint
μυλτιποιντ

11. type of signal that comprises voice transmission

analog
αναλογ

12. type of transmission in which data can be sent in both directions at the same time

full-duplex
φυλλ–δυπλεξ

13. range of frequencies that a communications channel can carry

bandwidth
βανδωιδτη

14. type of processor that is a computer dedicated to handling communications requirements of a larger system

front-end
φροντ–ενδ

15. checking connected terminals to see if they have data to send

polling
πολλινγ

16. allows commercial software to be accessed by many users

site license
σιτε λιχενσε

17. configuration of the equipment in a communications network

topology
τοπολογψ

18. devices connected to a network

nodes
νοδεσ

19. type of network that contains a central computer and one or more PCs or terminals connected to it

star
σταρ

20. a set of rules and procedures for exchanging information between computers

protocol
προτοχολ

The best PC modems and fiber-optic cables can transmit
τηε βεστ πχ μοδεμσ ανδ φιβερ – οπτιχ χαβλεσ χαν τρανσμιτ

thirty thousand single-spaced, typewritten pages in one
τηιρτψ τηουσανδ σινγλε–σπαχεδ, τψπεωριττεν παγεσ ιν ονε

second--literally faster than a speeding bullet.
σεχονδ □ λιτεραλλψ φαστερ τηαν α σπεεδινγ βυλλετ.

DISCOVERING COMPUTERS
A LINK TO THE FUTURE
WORLD WIDE WEB ENHANCED

CHAPTER 7
The Internet and the World Wide Web

CHAPTER OVERVIEW

This chapter provides an overview of the fastest growing area of computer technology: the Internet. The chapter begins with a definition of the Internet and a brief history of its origin. You learn about the World Wide Web, how Web pages work, the components of browser software. You are introduced to the use of multimedia on the Web, including virtual reality, and how search tools work. Intranets and firewalls are explained. Other Internet services are explained, including e-mail, FTP (file transfer protocol), Gopher, Telnet, Usenet, and Internet Relay Chat (IRC). Finally, you learn how to connect to the Internet and the World Wide Web.

CHAPTER OBJECTIVES

After completing this chapter, you will be able to:

- Describe the Internet and how it works

- Describe the World Wide Web portion of the Internet

- Understand how Web documents are linked to one another

- Understand how Web browser software works

- Describe several types of multimedia available on the Web

- Explain how to use a Web search tool to find information

- Describe different ways organizations use intranets and firewalls

- Explain how Internet services such as e-mail, FTP, Gopher, Telnet, Usenet, and Internet Relay Chat help you communicate and access information

- Describe how network computers are used

- Understand how to connect to the Internet and the World Wide Web

CHAPTER OUTLINE

  I. What is the Internet? [p. 7.2]

      When two or more networks are joined _____

(continued)

The term, the Internet (uppercase I), is used to describe _____

No single organization *owns* or controls the Internet.

II.　History of the Internet [p. 7.3]

The Internet began in 1969 as a network of four computers located _____

_____

The initial work was funded by _____

The first network thus was called _____

The Department of Defense had two major goals for the initial project. The first goal, _____

_____

In addition to the computer sites linked _____

III.　How the Internet works [p. 7.4]

The Internet operates by taking data _____

_____

The technique of breaking a message _____

_____

TCP/IP (transmission control protocol/Internet protocol) is _____

You can have access to the Internet through _____

A backbone is _____

Metropolitan area exchanges (MAEs), located in major cities, are used _____

_____

Internet traffic control is provided by routers, located throughout the Internet, which contain network maps. If the most direct path is overloaded _____

IV.　Internet addresses [p. 7.6]

The Internet relies on an addressing system.

Each location on the Internet has _____

The first part of the IP address _____

The second part of the IP address _____

The third part of the IP address _____

The fourth and last part of the IP address _____

A domain name is _____

Domain names are registered in _____

V.　The World Wide Web (WWW) [p. 7.7]

In 1991, Tim Berners-Lee at European Particle Physics Lab (CERN) released _____

_____

A hyperlink allows _____

_____

The collection of hyperlinked documents _____

A.　How a Web page works [p. 7.7]

A Web page is _____

_____

A hypertext document contains _____

A hypermedia document contains _____

Three types of hyperlinks exist:

1. _____ — _____

2. _____ — _____

3. _____ — _____

Web pages are created using _____

_____

B. Web browser software [p. 7.9]

Also called a Web browser, or simply a browser

Is a program that _____

The first Web browsers used _____

In 1993, Marc Andreessen created Mosaic, which _____

A home page is _____

A Uniform Resource Locator (URL) is _____

_____

URLs begin with _____

A history list _____

A bookmark and a history list allow _____

_____

Two widely used browsers are _____

C. Multimedia on the Web [p. 7.11]

Multimedia is the _____

Plug-ins run _____

Helper applications run _____

Java is _____

_____

Applets are _____

1. Graphics [p. 7.12]

Were the first media used to enhance the text-based Internet

2. Animation [p. 7.12]

Animation is used _____

_____

3. Audio [p. 7.13]

Must be downloaded before they can be played

Streaming audio allows _____

(continued)

Internet audioconferencing (Internet telephone service or Internet telephony) enables _____

_____

Internet voice mail enables _____

4.   Video [p. 7.14]

Video files, like audio, must be downloaded before they can be played.

Streaming video allows _____

_____

Videoconferencing over the Internet can be _____

5.   Virtual reality [p. 7.15]

Virtual reality (VR) is an artificial environment that you can experience.

On the Web, VR involves _____

_____

Most Web-based VR applications are developed using _____

D.   Searching for information on the Web [p. 7.16]

A search tool (search engine) is a _____

_____

Search tools search an index of _____

_____

VI.   Intranets and firewalls [p. 7.17]

Intranets are _____

Extranets are _____

A firewall is _____

A proxy server is _____

Caching involves _____

VII.   Other Internet services [p. 7.19]

Internet services include e-mail, FTP, Gopher, Telnet, Usenet, and Internet Chat Relay (IRC).

A.   E-mail [p. 7.19]

E-mail is _____

To receive e-mail you must _____

An Internet mailbox address is _____

_____

Your user name, or user-ID, must be different from other user names located on the same mailbox computer.

B.   FTP [p. 7.20]

FTP (file transfer protocol) is _____

_____

Computers that contain files available for FTP are called FTP sites or FTP servers.

Shareware software is _____

Anonymous FTP is _____

Archie sites are _____

Archie can be used to _____

An Archie gateway is _____

C. Gopher [p. 7.21]

Gopher is a _____

Gopher servers are _____

Unlike FTP and Archie, Gopher does not require _____

Most Gopher servers offer Veronica or Jughead _____

D. Telnet [p. 7.22]

Telnet is _____

A MUD (multiuser dimension) is a _____

_____

Another type of MUD, called a _____

_____

E. Usenet [p. 7.23]

Usenet is a collection of _____

A newsgroup is _____

A newsreader is _____

_____

A message is called _____

A posting is _____

A thread is _____

A moderator is _____

Netiquette (network etiquette) is _____

1. _____

_____

2. Read the FAQs. An FAQ is a list of frequently asked questions and their answers. FAQs are _____

_____

3. _____

4. _____

5. _____

6. Control your emotions. Sending an abusive message is called flaming and is considered inappropriate

_____

7. _____

F. Internet Relay Chat (IRC) [p. 7.24]

Internet Relay Chat, or IRC, allows _____

A channel is _____

A channel operator is _____

Use the /list command to _____

(continued)

Use the /join command to _____

VIII. Network computers [p. 7.25]

To reduce costs, many businesses and home users are turning to network computers.

A network computer, or NC, is _____

_____

Thin-client computers are _____

A. Network computers for business [p. 7.25]

For many business applications, a personal computer has more capability than the application requires.

Jobs that primarily involve entering transactions or looking up information in a database, do not _____

_____

Network computers for business reduce costs in several ways.

NCs are less expensive _____

_____

Software is easier _____

A network personal computer, or netPC, _____

_____

B. Network computers for the home [p. 7.26]

Sometimes called an information appliance, it is a _____

_____

To keep costs down, manufacturers _____

The set-top box uses _____

C. Summary of network computers [p. 7.27]

_____

_____

IX. How to Connect to the Internet and the World Wide Web [p. 7.28]

1. _____

Through _____

Through _____

Through _____

2. _____

3. _____

4. _____

5. _____

TERMS

absolute hyperlinks [p. 7.8]
Advanced Research Projects
  Agency (ARPA) [p. 7.3]
animation [p. 7.12]
anonymous FTP [p. 7.20]
applets [p. 7.11]
Archie [p. 7.20]
Archie gateway [p. 7.20]
Archie sites [p. 7.20]
ARPANET [p. 7.3]
article [p. 7.23]
audio [p. 7.13]

backbones [p. 7.5]
bookmark [p. 7.11]
browser [p. 7.9]

caching [p. 7.18]
channel [p. 7.25]
channel operator [p. 7.25]

domain name [p. 7.6]
domain name servers [p. 7.6]
domain name system (DNS)
  [p. 7.6]

e-mail [p. 7.19]
extranets [p. 7.17]

FAQ [p. 7.24]
firewall [p. 7.18]
flaming [p. 7.24]
FTP (file transfer protocol)
  [p. 7.20]
FTP servers [p. 7.20]
FTP sites [p. 7.20]

Gopher [p. 7.21]
Gopher servers [p. 7.21]
graphics [p. 7.12]

helper application [p. 7.11]
history list [p. 7.11]
home page [p. 7.10]
http:// [p. 7.10]
hyperlinks [p. 7.7]
hypermedia [p. 7.7]
hypertext [p. 7.7]
hypertext markup language
  (HTML) [p. 7.8]

hypertext transfer protocol [p.
  7.10]

information appliance [p. 7.26]
internet [p. 7.2]
the Internet [p. 7.2]
Internet audioconferencing
  [p. 7.13]
Internet mailbox address [p. 7.19]
Internet Relay Chat (IRC) [p. 7.25]
Internet service provider (ISP)
  [p. 7.28]
Internet telephone service [p. 7.13]
Internet telephony [p. 7.13]
Internet voice mail [p. 7.13]
internetwork [p. 7.2]
intranet [p. 7.17]
IP (Internet protocol) address
  [p. 7.6]
IRC [p. 7.25]

Java [p. 7.11]
/join [p. 7.25]
Jughead [p. 7.21]

/list [p. 7.25]

mailbox [p. 7.19]
markups [p. 7.8]
metropolitan area exchanges
  (MAEs) [p. 7.5]
moderator [p. 7.24]
MOO (multiuser object oriented)
  [p. 7.22]
Mosaic [p. 7.9]
MUD (multiuser dimension)
  [p. 7.22]

NC [p. 7.25]
netiquette [p. 7.24]
network computer [p. 7.25]
network personal computer
  [p. 7.26]
net PC [p. 7.26]
newbies [p. 7.24]
newsgroups [p. 7.23]
newsreader [p. 7.23]
NSFnet [p. 7.3]

online service [p. 7.28]

packets [p. 7.4]

plug-in [p. 7.11]
posting [p. 7.23]
PPP (point-to-point protocol)
  [p. 7.29]
proxy server [p. 7.18]

relative hyperlinks [p. 7.8]

search engine [p. 7.16]
search tool [p. 7.16]
set-top box [p. 7.26]
shareware [p. 7.20]
SHOUT! [p. 7.24]
SLIP (serial line Internet protocol)
  [p. 7.29]
spamming [p. 7.24]
streaming audio [p. 7.13]
streaming video [p. 7.14]

tags [p. 7.8]
target hyperlinks [p. 7.8]
TCP/IP (transmission control
  protocol/Internet protocol)
  [p. 7.4]
Telnet [p. 7.22]
thin-client [p. 7.25]
thread [p. 7.23]

Uniform Resource Locator (URL)
  [p. 7.10]
URL [p. 7.10]
Usenet [p. 7.23]
user name [p. 7.19]
user-ID [p. 7.19]

Veronica [p. 7.21]
video [p. 7.14]
virtual reality (VR) [p. 7.15]
VRML (virtual reality modeling
  language) [p. 7.15]

W3 [p. 7.7]
Web [p. 7.7]
Web browser [p. 7.9]
Web browser software [p. 7.9]
Web page [p. 7.7]
Web sites [p. 7.7]
Web surfing [p. 7.8]
welcome page [p. 7.10]
World Wide Web [p. 7.7]
WWW [p. 7.7]

SELF TEST
True/False

_____ 1. The term, the Internet, is used to describe two or more networks joined together.

_____ 2. The Internet works by taking data, dividing it into separate packets, and sending the packets along the best route available.

_____ 3. If the most direct path to a destination is overloaded, a router sends the packet along an alternate path.

_____ 4. Each Internet address has a three-part addressing system called the IP address.

_____ 5. The World Wide Web is the collection of all Internet network IP addresses controlled at a single location.

_____ 6. A browser retrieves a Web page by using the Uniform Resource Locator, which is an address that points to a specific resource on the Internet.

_____ 7. All virtual reality graphics and animation are constructed using HTML language.

_____ 8. Firewalls are used to deny network access to outsiders and to restrict employees' access to sensitive data.

_____ 9. The University of Wisconsin's Gopher was the first graphical interface Web browser.

_____ 10. In a newsgroup, an original message is called an article and adding a response of your own is called a thread.

Matching

1. _____ ARPANET

2. _____ TCP/IP

3. _____ backbones

4. _____ tags

5. _____ history list

6. _____ plug-in

7. _____ search tool

8. _____ proxy server

9. _____ FTP

10. _____ FAQ

a. records the pages you have viewed during a Web session

b. used to deny access to the network or sensitive data

c. high-speed communications lines

d. a software program that interprets and displays Web pages

e. frequently asked questions and their answers

f. an individual who reads newsgroup articles

g. a software program that finds Web sites

h. programmed to allow access to and from only specific network locations

i. guidelines for posting articles to newsgroups

j. Department of Defense Advanced Research Projects Agency Network

k. in HTML, special instructions that specify links to other documents and how the page is displayed

l. allows you to join others in real-time conversations

m. additional program that helps the browser run multimedia applications

n. an Internet standard that allows you to exchange files with other computers on the Internet

o. software used for packet switching on the Internet

Multiple Choice

_____ 1. What is the name for the technique that breaks a message into individual packets, sends the packets along the best route, and then reassembles the data at the destination?

    a.   TCP/IP

    b.   packet switching

    c.   protocol

    d.   transmission

_____ 2. What is an organization that has a permanent connection to the Internet and provides temporary connections for a fee?

    a.   World Wide Web

    b.   Metropolitan area exchange

    c.   backbone

    d.   Internet service provider

_____ 3. Where are domain names registered?

    a.   domain name server

    b.   domain name address

    c.   domain name system

    d.   domain name series

_____ 4. What is HTML (hypertext markup language)?

    a.   text hyperlinks to other documents

    b.   text, sound, and video connecting to other documents

    c.   a set of special software plug-ins used to hear audio and see animation

    d.   a set of special instructions, called tags, that specify how a document is displayed

_____ 5. What is the name of the page designated to be displayed each time you launch your browser?

    a.   home page

    b.   welcome page

    c.   Uniform Resource Locator

    d.   web page

_____ 6. What does a history list contain?

    a.   the title page of a web page and URL

    b.   the pages you have viewed during the time you are connected to the Web

    c.   the underlined text, as a different color, to indicate the previously viewed links

    d.   another name for hotlist or favorites list

_____ 7. Which of the following is _not_ considered an Internet service?

    a.   e-mail

    b.   FTP

    c.   terminal emulation software

    d.   Usenet

_____ 8. Which of the following Internet features is used to transfer files from one computer to another on the Internet?

    a.   FTP

    b.   Gopher

    c.   Telnet

    d.   Archie

(continued)

_____   9.   Which of the following is *not* part of netiquette?

      a.   choose your words carefully, because thousands of people may read your postings

      b.   choose a meaningful subject heading to give the reader a good idea of the contents of your article

      c.   use capital letters to indicate and emphasize important facts or features

      d.   post articles to appropriate newsgroups, do not spam, which is posting to several inappropriate newsgroups

_____   10.   A _____ is the name of a conversation group that is created on an Internet server for people to join.

      a.   gateway

      b.   channel

      c.   list

      d.   portal

Fill in the Blanks

1.   Each location on the Internet has a(n) _____ numeric address called an IP address.

2.   The first part of an IP address identifies the _____.

3.   The collection of hyperlinked documents accessible on the Internet has become known as _____.

4.   A(n) _____ is a hypertext or hypermedia document residing on an Internet computer that contains text, graphics, video, or sound.

5.   A(n) _____ is a program that interprets and displays Web pages and enables you to link to other Web pages.

6.   Technically, the first page at a Web site is called a(n) _____.

7.   A(n) _____ program runs multimedia within the browser window, while a helper application runs multimedia in a separate window.

8.   A programming language called _____ is being used to develop much of the multimedia on the Web.

9.   A(n) _____ is a software program that finds Web sites, Web pages, and Internet files that match one or more keywords that you enter.

10.   Anyone can log into a computer and transfer some, if not all, available files by using _____.

Complete the Table

Name	Web Site Location	Comments
Yahoo!	_____	One of the first. Updated daily.
_____	guide-p.infoseek.com	Searches Web or Usenet for words and phrases.
Lycos	_____	Comprehensive catalog plus multimedia content searches.
_____	www.altavista.digital.com	Creates indexes from more than 30 million Web pages.
Excite	_____	Concept-based search tool.
_____	www.webcrawler.com	Natural language search tool.
Four11	_____	Finds user-IDs.
_____	www.bigbook.com	Yellow pages for more than 16 million businesses.

Things to Think About

1. Today, experts estimate more than 12 million computers are connected and distribute information over the Internet. What needs or changes in technology have contributed to this colossal growth?

2. What was the original intention of the Internet and how has this changed? Can the Internet still be used for its original, intended purpose? What other purposes does or will the Internet serve?

3. Should access be restricted on the Internet? Who should decide? What kind of restrictions should be set in place? Should the Internet remain 'free'?

4. If restrictions are set in place, should that include censorship? What should be censored? What does the Constitution of the United States say about censorship on the Internet? How will we censor what is available in foreign countries?

Puzzle

Across

3. protocol used in address text box to find Web pages
5. Internet service provider
8. a program that finds Web sites based on keywords
11. protocol used to connect to the Internet
13. a role playing game in which one user plays against another
14. the protocol used to get files
16. an abbreviation for the collection of hyperlinked documents
18. a concept-based search engine or tool
19. one of the first search engines
21. commonly asked questions
22. a collection of news and discussion groups
23. an FTP search tool named after a comic strip character
24. the IP address that is placed in the address text box

Down

1. the text version of an IP address
2. used to move to other documents
4. protocol that enables one to access another computer
5. a worldwide group of connected networks
6. adding an article to a newsgroup
7. high-speed communications lines
9. the primary method of searching before search tools like Yahoo!
10. network of the Advance Research Projects Agency
12. an additional program used to run multimedia applications in the Web browser
15. a hypertext or hypermedia document
17. a program that interprets and displays Web pages
20. the language used to construct the Web page

SELF TEST ANSWERS

True/False	Matching	Multiple Choice
1. *F* [p. 7.2]	1. *j* [p. 7.3]	1. *b* [p. 7.4]
2. *T* [p. 7.4]	2. *o* [p. 7.4]	2. *d* [p. 7.5]
3. *T* [p. 7.5]	3. *c* [p. 7.5]	3. *c* [p. 7.6]
4. *F* [p. 7.6]	4. *k* [p. 7.8]	4. *d* [p. 7.8]
5. *F* [p. 7.7]	5. *a* [p. 7.11]	5. *a* [p. 7.10]
6. *T* [p. 7.10]	6. *m* [p. 7.11]	6. *b* [p. 7.11]
7. *F* [p. 7.15]	7. *g* [p. 7.16]	7. *c* [p. 7.19]
8. *T* [p. 7.18]	8. *h* [p. 7.18]	8. *a* [p. 7.20]
9. *F* [p. 7.21]	9. *n* [p. 7.20]	9. *c* [p. 7.24]
10. *F* [p. 7.23]	10. *e* [p. 7.24]	10. *b* [p. 7.24]

Fill in the Blanks

1. *four-part* [p. 7.6]

2. *geographic region* [p. 7.6]

3. the *World Wide Web (WWW, W3, or Web)* [p. 7.7]

4. *Web page* [p. 7.7]

5. *Web browser software, Web browser, or browser* [p. 7.9]

6. *welcome page* [p. 7.10]

7. *plug-in* [p. 7.11]

8. *Java* [p. 7.11]

9. *search tool or search engine* [p. 7.16]

10. *anonymous FTP* [p. 7.20]

Complete the Table [p. 7.17]

Name	Web Site Location	Comments
Yahoo!	*www.yahoo.com*	One of the first. Updated daily.
Infoseek	guide-p.infoseek.com	Searches Web or Usenet for words and phrases.
Lycos	*www.lycos.com*	Comprehensive catalog plus multimedia content searches.
AltaVista	www.altavista.digital.com	Creates indexes from more than 30 million Web pages.
Excite	*www.excite.com*	Concept-based search tool.
WebCrawler	www.webcrawler.com	Natural language search tool.
Four11	*www.Four11.com*	Finds user-IDs.
BigBook	www.bigbook.com	Yellow pages for more than 16 million businesses.

Puzzle Answer

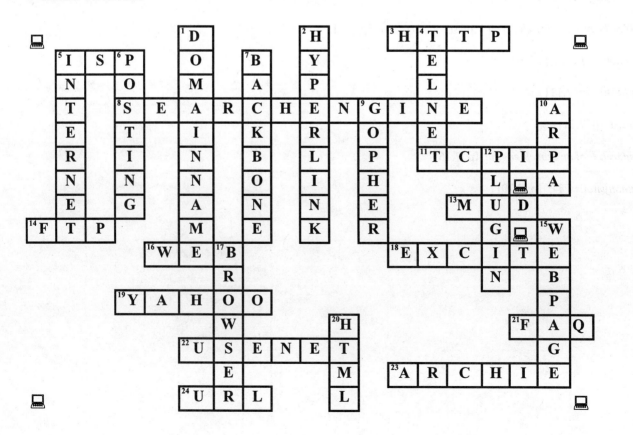

C H A P T E R   8
Operating Systems and System Software

CHAPTER OVERVIEW

This chapter discusses operating system features of both large and small computer systems. System software is defined, and the three major categories of system software are identified. You learn what an operating system is and how an operating system is loaded into memory. Several types of operating systems are explained, and the functions of an operating system are detailed. A variety of popular operating systems is described. Finally, you discover the purpose of utility programs and language translators.

CHAPTER OBJECTIVES

After completing this chapter, you will be able to:

• Describe the three major categories of system software

• Define the term operating system

• Describe the functions of an operating system

• Understand what happens when an operating system is loaded

• Explain the difference between proprietary and portable operating systems

• Name and briefly describe the major operating systems that are being used today

• Discuss utilities and language translators

CHAPTER OUTLINE

I.   What is system software? [p. 8.2]

System software consists of _____

_____

Can be classified into three major categories: _____, _____, and

_____

(continued)

II. What is an operating system? [p. 8.2]

An operating system (OS) is a set of _____
_____

Usually stored on hard disk drive

The essential and more frequently used instructions are stored in the computer's memory and is called the resident portion.

Names for resident portion: _____, _____,
_____, _____, _____, and
_____

Internal commands are _____

External commands are _____

The nonresident portion of the operating system remains _____
_____

The user interface is _____

The three types of user interfaces are _____, _____, and
_____

Using a command-line user interface, _____
_____

Command language is _____

A menu-driven user interface _____

A graphical user interface (GUI) _____

Icons are _____

Today, many graphical user interfaces incorporate browser-like features, which make them even easier to use.

III. Functions of an operating system [p. 8.4]

The operating system performs four functions that allow you and the application software to interact with the computer: _____, _____, _____, and
_____

A. Process management [p. 8.4]

A process (task) is _____
_____

1. Single tasking [p. 8.4]

Single tasking operating systems allow _____

If one program is loaded in memory and you wish to work on another application, you must exit the first program and load the second into memory.

2. Multitasking [p. 8.4]

Multitasking operating systems _____

Multiuser timesharing operating systems _____

Multitasking is accomplished in three ways: _____, _____,
and _____

With context switching, _____

The operating system saves information _____

With cooperative multitasking, _____

_____

With preemptive multitasking, _____

_____

A time slice is _____

If two or more processes have the same priority, _____

_____

Some multitasking operating systems permit multithreading, which is _____

_____

A thread is _____

Multithreading allows _____

_____

A process is in the foreground if _____

A process is in the background if _____

3. Multiprocessing [p. 8.6]

Computers that have more than one CPU are called multiprocessors.

Multiprocessing operating systems coordinate _____

Asymmetric multiprocessing is _____

Symmetric multiprocessing is _____

A unique advantage of _____

A fault-tolerant computer is _____

B. Memory management [p. 8.7]

During processing, some areas of memory are used _____

_____

Other areas of memory _____

_____

Buffers are _____

Partitions are _____

Virtual memory management increases _____

_____

A swap file is _____

The most common way operating systems perform virtual memory management is by using a process called paging. With paging _____

The size of a page, or frame, _____

Swapping is _____

C. Input and output management [p. 8.8]

The operating system is responsible for managing the input and output processes. The operating system manages _____

(continued)

With spooling, _____

_____

The terms *spool* and *spooling* _____

_____

Device drivers are _____

Plug and Play technology _____

D. System administration [p. 8.10]

_____

_____

1. System performance [p. 8.10]

    System performance usually is gauged by the user in terms of response time.

    Response time is _____

    Response time varies based on _____

    CPU utilization is _____

    Thrashing is _____

    _____

2. System security [p. 8.11]

    Most multiuser operating systems allow _____

    A logon code _____

    A user ID _____

    A password _____

    Both successful and unsuccessful logons are stored in a file that can be used to _____

    _____

3. Disk and file management [p. 8.11]

    Some of the disk and file management functions include _____

    _____

IV. Loading an operating system [p. 8.12]

The process of loading the operating system into memory is called booting the system.

The following steps explain what occurs during the boot process on a personal computer using Windows 95:

1. _____

2. _____

3. _____

4. _____

5. _____

6. _____

7. _____

8. _____

9. _____

V. Popular operating systems [p. 8.14]

First operating systems were developed by manufacturers specifically for computers in their product line.

These operating systems, called proprietary operating systems, were _____

Today, the trend is _____

The advantage of portable operating systems _____

Upward compatible _____

Downward compatible _____

   A. DOS [p. 8.14]

       DOS (Disk Operating System) refers to _____

       Microsoft developed PC-DOS (Personal Computer DOS) for _____

       Microsoft marketed and sold _____

       DOS is no longer the top-selling operating system because _____

       _____

   B. Windows 3.x [p. 8.15]

       Windows 3.x refers to three _____

       An operating environment is _____

       A shell acts as _____

   C. Windows 95 and beyond [p. 8.16]

       Windows 95 is a true operating system because _____

       One advantage of Windows 95 is _____

       Another advantage _____

       A frame is _____

       _____

   D. Windows CE [p. 8.16]

       _____

       _____

   E. Windows NT [p. 8.17]

       Windows NT, or simply NT, is _____

       NT uses a modular design.

       The central module, called _____

       _____

       Features include:

        • _____

        • _____

        • _____

        • _____

        • _____

(continued)

F.   Macintosh [p. 8.17]

_____

_____

Distinctive features of MacOS include _____, _____,

and _____

G.   OS/2 [p. 8.18]

_____

_____

The latest version of OS/2, called OS/2 Warp 4, includes:

 • _____

 • _____

 • _____

 • _____

 • _____

 • _____

H.   UNIX [p. 8.18]

_____

_____

UNIX does have some weaknesses, such as _____

_____

_____

I.   NetWare [p. 8.19]

NetWare from Novell is a widely used network operating system designed for client-server networks.

_____

_____

VI. Utilities [p. 8.19]

Utility programs perform _____

_____

Some of the frequently performed tasks of utility programs:

 • File viewer _____

 • File conversion _____

 • File compression _____

 • Backup _____

 • Diagnostics _____

 • Uninstaller _____

 • Antivirus _____

 • Screen saver _____

 • Desktop enhancer _____

 • Internet organizer _____

VII. Language translators [p. 8.23]

Language translators are _____

_____

VIII. Summary of operating systems and system software [p. 8.23]

_____

_____

TERMS

antivirus program [p. 8.21]
asymmetric multiprocessing
    [p. 8.6]
AUTOEXEC.BAT [p. 8.13]

background [p. 8.5]
backup software [p. 8.20]
Basic Input/Output System
    [p. 8.12]
BIOS [p. 8.12]
booting [p. 8.12]
buffers [p. 8.7]

command language [p. 8.3]
command-line user interface
    [p. 8.3]
CONFIG.SYS [p. 8.13]
context switching [p. 8.5]
control program [p. 8.2]
cooperative multitasking [p. 8.5]
CPU utilization [p. 8.10]

desktop enhancer [p. 8.22]
device drivers [p. 8.9]
diagnostic program [p. 8.21]
DOS (Disk Operating System)
    [p. 8.14]
downward compatible [p. 8.14]

executive [p. 8.2]
external commands [p. 8.2]

fault-tolerant computer
    [p. 8.6]
file compression software
    [p. 8.20]
file conversion [p. 8.20]
file viewer [p. 8.19]
foreground [p. 8.5]
frames [p. 8.16]

graphical user interface (GUI)
    [p. 8.3]

internal commands [p. 8.2]

Internet organizer [p. 8.22]
kernel [p. 8.2]

language translators [p. 8.23]
logon code [p. 8.11]
Macintosh [p. 8.17]
MacOS [p. 8.17]
master program [p. 8.2]
menu-driven user interface
    [p. 8.13]
monitor [p. 8.2]
MS-DOS (Microsoft DOS)
    [p. 8.14]
multiprocessing operating system
    [p. 8.6]
multiprocessors [p. 8.6]
multitasking [p. 8.4]
multithreading [p. 8.5]
multiuser timesharing [p. 8.4]

NetWare [p. 8.19]
NT [p. 8.17]

operating environment
    [p. 8.15]
operating system (OS) [p. 8.2]
OS/2 [p. 8.18]

page [p. 8.7]
paging [p. 8.7]
partitions [p. 8.7]
password [p. 8.11]
PC-DOS (Personal Computer
    DOS) [p. 8.14]
Plug and Play technology [p. 8.9]
portable operating systems
    [p. 8.14]
POST [p. 8.12]
Power On Self Test [p. 8.12]
preemptive multitasking [p. 8.5]
print spool [p. 8.9]
process [p. 8.4]

proprietary operating systems
    [p. 8.14]
registry [p. 8.13]
response time [p. 8.10]

screen saver [p. 8.22]
shell [p. 8.15]
single tasking [p. 8.4]
spooling [p. 8.9]
supervisor [p. 8.2]
swap file [p. 8.7]
swapping [p. 8.8]
symmetric multiprocessing
    [p. 8.6]
system software [p. 8.2]

task [p. 8.4]
thrashing [p. 8.10]
time slice [p. 8.5]

uninstaller [p. 8.21]
UNIX [p. 8.18]
upward compatible [p. 8.14]
user ID [p. 8.11]
user interface [p. 8.2]
utility programs [p. 8.19]

virtual memory management
    [p. 8.7]
virus [p. 8.21]

Win 95 [p. 8.16]
Windows 3.0 [p. 8.15]
Windows 3.1 [p. 8.15]
Windows 3.x [p. 8.15]
Windows 95 [p. 8.16]
Windows CE [p. 8.16]
Windows for Workgroups
    [p. 8.15]
Windows NT [p. 8.17]

SELF TEST

True/False

_____ 1. Some of the functions of the operating system include starting up the computer; loading, executing, and storing application programs; and storing and retrieving files.

_____ 2. Commands that are included in the resident portion of the operating system are called external commands.

_____ 3. In asymmetric multiprocessing, application tasks may be assigned to whatever CPU is available.

_____ 4. Fault-tolerant computer systems are used for airline reservation systems, communications networks, bank teller machines, and other applications where it is important to keep the computer operating at all times.

_____ 5. Response time is a fixed amount of CPU processing time, usually measured in milliseconds (thousandths of a second).

_____ 6. The process of loading an operating system into memory is called spooling.

_____ 7. The BIOS, a set of instructions that provides the interface between the operating system and the hardware, is stored in a read-only memory (ROM) chip.

_____ 8. Many computer users are supporting the move away from portable operating systems, which will run on many manufacturers' computers, toward proprietary (or privately owned operating systems).

_____ 9. Today, most major computer manufacturers offer a multiuser version of the UNIX operating system to run on their computers.

_____ 10. Utility programs perform specific tasks related to managing computer resources or files.

Matching

1. _____ DOS
2. _____ MS-DOS
3. _____ PC-DOS
4. _____ Windows
5. _____ Windows CE
6. _____ Windows NT
7. _____ Macintosh
8. _____ OS/2
9. _____ UNIX
10. _____ NetWare

a. marketed directly by Microsoft and sold to makers of IBM-compatible personal computer systems

b. widely used network operating system designed for client-server networks

c. the first widely used graphical user interface for IBM-compatible personal computers

d. operating system used on larger IBM mainframe computers

e. first commercially successful graphical user interface, set the standard for ease of use

f. the primary operating system for personal computers in the 1970s

g. a multiuser, multitasking operating system developed by Bell Laboratories in the early 1970s

h. IBM's virtual machine operating system

i. IBM's operating system designed to work with 32-bit microprocessors

j. proprietary operating system designed to work on Tandy TRS-80 personal computers

k.   designed for use on client-server computer systems; requires significant system resources

l.   proprietary operating system for Apple II series of microcomputers

m.   developed by Microsoft for IBM and installed by IBM on systems sold by IBM

n.   designed for use on wireless communication devices and smaller computers, such as hand-helds and palmtops

o.   at one time, the most widely used operating system on personal computers

Multiple Choice

1.   Which of the following functions is *not* performed by system software?
   a.   starting up the computer
   b.   telling the computer how to produce information
   c.   loading, executing, and storing application programs
   d.   storing and retrieving files

2.   What is the nonresident portion of the operating system?
   a.   the portion of the operating system that must be stored in the memory of the computer for the computer to operate
   b.   the portion of the operating system that contains the essential and most frequently used commands
   c.   the portion of the operating system that remains on disk and is available to be loaded into memory when needed
   d.   the portion of the operating system that carries out command language instructions

3.   What are the four functions performed by an operating system?
   a.   allocating system resources, monitoring system activity, and disk and file management
   b.   process management, memory management, input and output management, and system administration
   c.   formatting disks, copying disks, and deleting files
   d.   measuring system performance, ensuring system security, and implementing applications

4.   In which process management function is multithreading used?
   a.   single tasking
   b.   multiprocessing
   c.   multitasking
   d.   virtual machine

5.   What process management technique assigns application processes to whatever CPU is available?
   a.   multithreading
   b.   multiprocessing
   c.   symmetric
   d.   asymmetric

(continued)

_____ 6. What are the areas in memory where data is stored that has just been read from an input device or is waiting to be sent to an output device?

     a. buffers

     b. partitions

     c. segments

     d. pages

_____ 7. What is thrashing?

     a. the process of loading the operating system into memory

     b. a situation where a report is first written (saved) to disk before it is printed

     c. the process of making room for new data or instructions by writing back to disk one or more of the pages or segments currently in memory

     d. a situation where the system spends more time moving pages to and from the disk than processing data

_____ 8. What is a portable operating system?

     a. an operating system developed by manufacturers for computers in their product line

     b. a privately owned operating system

     c. an operating system that will run on many manufacturers' computers

     d. an operating system that combines separate procedures and data used by most programs

_____ 9. Early versions of which operating system are not technically operating systems, but rather are graphical user interface operating environments that work in combination with an operating system?

     a. Windows

     b. Macintosh

     c. OS/2

     d. NetWare

_____ 10. The Restore program works in conjunction with the backup utility. What function does it provide?

     a. configures a system to make the most memory available for running applications

     b. allows the user to select one or more files for copying to disks or tape

     c. allows the user to reload the copied files to another storage medium

     d. reduces the amount of space that a file requires

Fill in the Blanks

1. _____ can be classified into three major categories: operating systems, utilities, and language translators.

2. The programs in the _____ function as an interface between the user, the application programs, and the computer hardware.

3. _____ operating systems, the first type of operating systems developed, allow only one user to run one program at one time.

4. Multitasking operating systems that can support more than one user running the same program are sometimes called _____ operating systems.

5. Operating systems allocate at least some portion of memory into fixed areas called _____.

6. _____ increases the amount of memory the operating system can use by allocating a set amount of disk space to be used to store items during processing, in addition to the existing memory.

7. Most multiuser operating systems provide for a(n) _____, which usually identifies the application that will be used.

8. The advantage of _____ operating systems, such as DOS, is that the user is not tied to a particular manufacturer.

9. Like an operating environment, a(n) _____ acts as an interface between the user and the operating system.

10. Special-purpose system software programs called _____ are used to convert the programming instructions written by programmers into the binary code that a computer can understand.

Complete the Table

Operating System Process Management	
	Single user can run one program at a time
Multitasking	
Context switching	
	Programs switch when they reach a logical break point
Preemptive multitasking	
	Multiple CPUs
Asymmetric multiprocessing	Tasks assigned to specific CPUs; each CPU has its own memory

Things to Think About

1. Why is the operating system usually stored on disk?

2. Because most people can do only one thing at a time, what is the value of a multitasking operating system?

3. Although the same functions apply to all operating systems, these functions become more complex for operating systems that allow more than one program to run at a time. Why?

4. Why are various system security measures provided by most multiuser operating systems?

Puzzle

All of the words described below appear in the puzzle. Words either may be forward or backward, across, up and down, or diagonal. Circle each word as you find it.

```
R E S P O N S E T I M E
B I O S P O O L I N G X
A T C C D P P A M V S T
C H I R S O A N E M R E
K R R E W R S R S E E R
G A T E A T S E L T F N
R S E N P A W T I S F A
O H M S P B O N C Y U L
U I M A I L R I E S B T
N N Y V N E D L L E H S
D G S E G N I T O O B O
E M A R F L E N R E K P
```

type of software that consists of all the programs related to controlling the operations of the computer equipment

for PCs using DOS, name for resident portion of the operating system

commands included in the resident portion of the operating system

commands in nonresident portion of the operating system

process of loading an operating system into memory

set of instructions that provides the interface between the operating system and hardware devices

tests that check to make sure the computer system equipment is working correctly

type of multiprocessing in which application tasks are assigned to a specific CPU

abbreviation for type of operating system that allows a single computer to run two or more different operating systems

fixed amount of CPU processing time, usually measured in milliseconds

type of jobs that receive a lower processing priority and less CPU time

areas in memory where data just read from an input device or waiting to be sent to an output device is stored

in virtual memory management, process of making room for new data by writing back to disk pages or segments

writing a report back to disk before it is printed

interval from the moment a user enters data until the computer responds

situation where the system spends more time moving pages than processing data

usually confidential, known only to the user and computer system administrator

type of operating system that will run on many manufacturers' computers

the most widely used operating system on personal computers

program that acts as an interface between the user and the operating system

program that prevents ghosting (a dim version of an image permanently etched on the monitor screen)

SELF TEST ANSWERS

True/False

1. *T* [p. 8.2]
2. *F* [p. 8.2]
3. *F* [p. 8.6]
4. *T* [p. 8.6]
5. *F* [p. 8.10]
6. *F* [p. 8.12]
7. *T* [p. 8.12]
8. *F* [p. 8.14]
9. *T* [p. 8.18]
10. *T* [p. 8.19]

Matching

1. *o* [p. 8.14]
2. *a* [p. 8.14]
3. *m* [p. 8.14]
4. *c* [p. 8.15]
5. *n* [p. 8.16]
6. *k* [p. 8.17]
7. *e* [p. 8.17]
8. *i* [p. 8.18]
9. *g* [p. 8.18]
10. *b* [p. 8.19]

Multiple Choice

1. *b* [p. 8.2]
2. *c* [p. 8.2]
3. *b* [p. 8.4]
4. *c* [p. 8.5]
5. *c* [p. 8.6]
6. *a* [p. 8.7]
7. *d* [p. 8.10]
8. *c* [p. 8.14]
9. *a* [p. 8.15]
10. *c* [p. 8.20]

Fill in the Blanks

1. *System software* [p. 8.2]
2. *operating system* [p. 8.2]
3. *Single tasking* [p. 8.4]
4. *multiuser timesharing* [p. 8.4]
5. *partitions* [p. 8.7]
6. *Virtual memory management* [p. 8.7]
7. *logon code* [p. 8.11]
8. *portable* [p. 8.14]
9. *shell* [p. 8.15]
10. *language translators* [p. 8.23]

Complete the Table [p. 8.4]

Operating System Process Management	
Single Tasking	Single user can run one program at a time
Multitasking	*Multiple programs can run*
Context switching	*User switches back and forth between programs*
Cooperative multitasking	Programs switch when they reach a logical break point
Preemptive multitasking	*Operating system switches programs based* *on allocated amount of time and priority*
Multiprocessing	Multiple CPUs
Asymmetric multiprocessing	Tasks assigned to specific CPUs; each CPU has its own memory
Symmetric multiprocessing	*Tasks assigned to available CPUs; CPUs share* *memory*

Puzzle Answer

C H A P T E R 9
Data Management and Databases

CHAPTER OVERVIEW

The purpose of this chapter is to explain the need for data management, how files on secondary storage are organized and maintained (kept current), and the advantages, organization, and use of databases. First, data management is introduced. Files, types of file organization, and the maintenance of data in files are explained. You discover what a database is, why databases are a better way to organize and manage data, and the advantages of a database system. Database organization, database management systems, and query languages are described.

CHAPTER OBJECTIVES

After completing this chapter, you will be able to:

• Discuss data management and explain why it is needed

• Describe the hierarchy of data

• Describe sequential files, indexed files, and direct files

• Explain the difference between sequential and random organization and retrieval of records from a file

• Describe the data maintenance procedures for updating data, including adding, changing, and deleting

• Discuss the advantages of a database management system (DBMS)

• Describe hierarchical, network, relational, and object-oriented database systems

• Explain the use of a query language

• Describe the responsibilities of a database administrator

• Explain several guidelines for creating database files

• Discuss personal computer database systems

CHAPTER OUTLINE

I. Data management [p. 9.2]

   Refers to _____

   _____

(continued)

The purpose of data management is _____
_____

 A. Data accuracy [p. 9.3]

  Data accuracy (data integrity) means _____
  _____

  Data must be reliable and timely.

 B. Data security [p. 9.3]

  Involves _____

  Backup refers to _____

 C. Data maintenance [p. 9.3]

  Refers to _____

  Maintaining data is called updating and includes procedures for _____ ,

  _____ , and _____ data

II. The hierarchy of data [p. 9.4]

 • A bit is _____

 • A byte is _____

 • A field is _____

  The key field or key is _____

 • A record is _____

 • A file is _____

 • A database is _____

III. Types of file organization [p. 9.5]

 A file can be organized in one of three ways: _____ , _____ , and

 _____

 A. Sequential file organization [p. 9.5]

  Sequential file organization means _____
  _____

  Sequential retrieval (sequential access) means _____
  _____

  Major disadvantage of sequential retrieval is _____

  Sequential retrieval is appropriate when _____

 B. Indexed file organization [p. 9.6]

  Indexed file organization uses _____
  _____

  An index consists of _____

  Records can be accessed both sequentially and direct.

  Direct or random access means _____
  _____

  An advantage of indexed files is _____

A disadvantage of indexed files is _____

C. Direct file organization [p. 9.7]

Direct file organization (relative or random file organization) uses _____

_____

Buckets are _____

Buckets can be divided _____

Hashing is _____

The hashing technique creates a problem because _____

_____

Synonyms are _____

A collision is _____

In a direct file, records can be retrieved either _____

Steps in retrieving a record from a direct file:

1. _____

2. _____

3. _____

To retrieve records sequentially _____

_____

D. Summary of file organization concepts [p. 9.8]

Sequential file organization is _____

Indexed and direct file organization is _____

IV. How is data in files maintained? [p. 9.9]

Data maintenance or updating involves _____

A. Adding records [p. 9.9]

Records are added to a file when _____

B. Changing records [p. 9.10]

Changing data takes place for two primary reasons: (1) _____, and
(2) _____

C. Deleting records [p. 9.11]

Records are deleted when _____

D. Summary of how data is maintained [p. 9.12]

Data maintenance is essential for _____

V. Databases: a better way to manage and organize data [p. 9.12]

Data (and the information it represents) is one of an organization's more valuable assets.

Databases are implemented to organize information resources and provide for timely and efficient access.

VI. What is a database? [p. 9.12]

In file-oriented systems, a flat file is _____

_____

(continued)

A file management system (flat-file management system) is _____

_____

The term database means _____

A database management system (DBMS) is _____

_____

VII. Why use a database? [p. 9.13]

Files in a file-oriented system are independent of one another, often creating duplicate data.

Advantages a DBMS offers over a file-oriented system:

- _____

- _____

- _____

- _____

- _____

VIII. Types of database organization [p. 9.15]

A. Hierarchical database [p. 9.15]

In a hierarchical database, _____

_____

Branches of the tree are made _____

Disadvantages: _____

_____

Advantage: _____

A hierarchical file system is the file system used on most PCs.

The root directory is _____

Subdirectories or folders are _____

A path is _____

B. Network database [p. 9.16]

A network database is _____

A member is _____

An owner is _____

C. Relational database [p. 9.17]

In a relational database, _____

_____

Tables are divided into _____

A domain is _____

Advantages: _____

_____

Disadvantage: _____

D. Object-oriented database [p. 9.18]

An object-oriented database _____

_____

_____

IX. Database management systems [p. 9.18]

Common features of a DBMS:

- _____

- _____

- _____

- _____

- _____

- _____

X. Query languages: access to the database [p. 9.20]

A query language is _____

_____

Query-by-example (QBE) _____

A. Querying a relational database [p. 9.21]

A view, or subset, is created _____

Relational operations are used to query a relational database

The three relational operations are:

- _____ – _____

- _____ – _____

- _____ – _____

B. Structured query language [p. 9.22]

_____

_____

XI. Database administration [p. 9.22]

The centralization of data into a database requires cooperation and coordination on the part of the database users.

A. The role of the database administrator [p. 9.23]

The database administrator (DBA) is _____

Responsibilities:

- _____

- _____

- _____

- _____

- _____

- _____

B. The role of the user in a database system [p. 9.24]

_____

_____

(continued)

C. Guidelines for designing database files [p. 9.25]

For relational databases, a process called normalization is _____

_____

Database file guidelines:

_____

_____

_____

_____

_____

XII. Summary of data management and databases [p. 9.25]

_____

_____

TERMS

access privileges [p. 9.18]
attribute [p. 9.4, 9.17]

backup [p. 9.3]
backward recovery [p. 9.19]
bit [p. 9.4]
BLOB (binary large object)
   [p. 9.5]
buckets [p. 9.7]
byte [p. 9.4]

child record [p. 9.15]
collision [p. 9.8]

data accuracy [p. 9.3]
data dictionary [p. 9.18]
data integrity [p. 9.3]
data maintenance [p. 9.3]
data mart [p. 9.26]
data mining [p. 9.26]
data security [p. 9.3]
data warehouse [p. 9.26]
database [p. 9.5, 9.12]
database administrator [p. 9.23]
database management system
   (DBMS) [p. 9.12]
DBA [p. 9.23]
direct access [p. 9.6]
direct file organization [p. 9.7]
domain [p. 9.17]

field [p. 9.4]
file [p. 9.4]

file management system
   [p. 9.12]
flat files [p. 9.12]
folder [p. 9.16]
forward recovery [p. 9.19]

hashing [p. 9.7]
hierarchical database [p. 9.15]
hierarchical file system [p. 9.16]

index [p. 9.6]
indexed file organization
   [p. 9.6]

join relational operation
   [p. 9.21]

key [p. 9.4]
key field [p. 9.4]

member [p. 9.16]

network database [p. 9.16]
normalization [p. 9.25]

object-oriented database
   [p. 9.18]
owner [p. 9.16]

parent record [p. 9.15]
path [p. 9.16]
prime number [p. 9.7]
project relational operation
   [p. 9.21]

query [p. 9.14]
query by example (QBE)
   [p. 9.20]

query language [p. 9.19, 9.20]
random access [p. 9.6]
record [p. 9.4]
relational database [p. 9.17]
relational operations [p. 9.21]
relations [p. 9.17]
reliable data entry [p. 9.3]
replication [p. 9.19]
rollback [p. 9.19]
rollforward [p. 9.19]
root directory [p. 9.16]
root record [p. 9.15]

select relational operation
   [p. 9.21]
sequential file organization
   [p. 9.5]
slots [p. 9.7]
SQL [p. 9.22]
Structured Query Language
   [p. 9.22]
subdirectory [p. 9.16]
synonyms [p. 9.8]

tables [p. 9.17]
timely data [p. 9.3]
tuples [p. 9.17]

updating [p. 9.3]
utility programs [p. 9.18]

view [p. 9.21]

SELF TEST
True/False

_____ 1. Backup, a part of data security, refers to using a log to reverse transactions that took place during a certain period of time, such as an hour.

_____ 2. Sequential file organization means the system can go directly to a record without having to read the preceding records.

_____ 3. A disadvantage of indexed files is that searching an index for a record in a large file can take a long time and maintaining one or more indexes adds to the processing time whenever a record is added, changed, or deleted.

_____ 4. The maintenance of data is essential for generating reliable information.

_____ 5. The advantage of a file-oriented system is that each file is independent, which saves secondary storage space and allows data to be maintained more easily.

_____ 6. Records located in separate branches of a hierarchical database can be accessed easily at the same time.

_____ 7. Most database management systems include a feature called query-by-example (QBE) that helps you construct a query by displaying a list of fields available in the file from which the query will be made.

_____ 8. The database administrator (DBA) is responsible for database design, user coordination, performance monitoring, system security, data distribution, and backup and recovery.

_____ 9. Normalization is a process used to organize data into the most efficient and logical file relationships.

_____ 10. One database file guideline is to create fields for information that can be derived from entries in other fields.

Matching

1. _____ sequential file organization
2. _____ indexed file organization
3. _____ direct file organization
4. _____ database management system
5. _____ file management system
6. _____ hierarchical database
7. _____ network database
8. _____ relational database
9. _____ object-oriented database
10. _____ query language

a. records stored one after the other, normally in ascending or descending order, based on a value in the key field

b. data is organized in tables that are further divided into rows (tuples) and fields (attributes)

c. uses the key value of a record to determine the location on disk where the record is stored

d. procedures used to keep data accurate and timely and provide for security and maintenance

e. has a list containing the values of one or more fields and the corresponding disk address for each record

f. the software that allows a user to create, maintain, and access one file at a time

g. structured groups of related facts that make up files

h. data is organized like a family tree or organization chart

i. process used to organize data into the most efficient and logical file relationships

j. keeps track of entities that contain both data and the action to be taken on the data

k. independent and contains all the information necessary to process records in that file

l. simple English-like communication that allows users to specify what data they want to see

(continued)

m.   process of using a formula and performing the calculation to determine the location of a record

n.   similar to a hierarchical database except each child record can have more than one parent

o.   the software that allows you to create, maintain, and report data and file relationships

Multiple Choice

_____   1. What aspect of data management refers to the procedures to keep data current?
   a.   data accuracy
   b.   data integrity
   c.   data security
   d.   data maintenance

_____   2. Sequential retrieval would be most appropriate in an application used to do which of the following?
   a.   locate specific library references
   b.   update an individual student file
   c.   print a company's weekly payroll checks
   d.   display sales orders for a particular customer

_____   3. How is indexed file organization different from sequential file organization?
   a.   in sequential file organization, records are stored in ascending or descending order based on the value in the key field of the record
   b.   in indexed file organization, a list is maintained containing the values of a field and the corresponding disk address for each record
   c.   in sequential file organization, a formula and the appropriate calculation is used to determine the location of a record
   d.   in indexed file organization, records can be accessed randomly, but they cannot be accessed sequentially

_____   4. Why are records added to a file?
   a.   when additional data is needed to make the file current
   b.   to correct data that is known to be incorrect
   c.   to update data when new data becomes available
   d.   when records are no longer needed as data

_____   5. One of the advantages of a database system is reduced data redundancy. What other advantage is most closely related to reduced data redundancy?
   a.   improved data accuracy
   b.   easier reporting
   c.   improved data security
   d.   reduced development time

_____   6. Which type of database does *not* have data relationships defined when the database is created?
   a.   hierarchical database
   b.   network database
   c.   relational database
   d.   all of the above

_____ 7. What does the select relational operation do?
    a.   chooses certain records based on user-supplied criteria
    b.   reenters records from the last time the system was backed up
    c.   specifies the fields that appear on the query output
    d.   combines two files

_____ 8. Which of the following is usually a responsibility of the database administrator (DBA)?
    a.   database design and user coordination
    b.   backup and recovery
    c.   system security and performance monitoring
    d.   all of the above

_____ 9. For relational database files, what is normalization?
    a.   a process used to organize data into the most efficient and logical file relationships
    b.   restoring a database in the event of a hardware or software malfunction
    c.   a process to determine the location of a record by using a formula and calculation
    d.   manipulating the data from one or more files to create a unique view of the total data

_____ 10. Which database file guideline would be followed by calculating a person's age from the birth date?
    a.   set default values for frequently entered fields
    b.   do not create fields for information that can be derived from entries in other fields
    c.   allow enough space for each field
    d.   use separate fields for logically distinct items

Fill in the Blanks

1. The purpose of _____ is to ensure that data required for an application will be available in the correct form and at the proper time for processing.

2. Updating includes procedures for _____ obsolete data, such as removing inactive records.

3. A(n) _____ is a collection of related records or data stored under a single name.

4. _____ retrieval has a major disadvantage: because records must be retrieved in the same order as they are stored, the only way to retrieve a record is to read all the preceding records.

5. A(n) _____ consists of a list containing the values of one or more fields and the corresponding disk address for each record in a file.

6. The term _____ usually means a collection of related files stored together.

7. Like a family tree, the _____ has branches made up of parent and child records, with each child record having only one parent record.

8. In network database terminology, a parent record is referred to as a(n) _____.

9. The three _____ allow the user to manipulate the data from one or more files to create a unique view, or subset, of the total data.

10. In small organizations, the _____ usually is responsible for the overall management of computer resources, in addition to the management of all database activities.

Complete the Table

FEATURE	DESCRIPTION
Data Dictionary	
_____	Creates files and dictionaries, monitors performance, copies data, and deletes unwanted records
Security	
_____	Distributes data to other computers
Recovery	
_____	Creates views and specifies report content and format

Things to Think About

1. Why is sequential file organization used on tape, while indexed and direct files are stored on disk?

2. Why would records be flagged so they are not processed, instead of being immediately deleted (physically removed from storage)?

3. Although a database management system offers improved data security, some claim that if security is breached, data is more vulnerable than in a file management system. Why?

4. When designing a database file, why should large groups of data probably be separate files?

Puzzle

The terms described by each phrase below are written in code. Break the code by writing the correct term above the coded word. Then, use your broken code to translate the final sentence.

1. includes procedures for adding, changing, and deleting data

updating
◆□✳◕▼✳■✳

2. collection of related data or information stored under a single name

✳✳●✳

3. structured groups of related facts

□✳✳□□✳▲

4. individual facts that make up records

✳✳✳●✳▲

5. location in a direct file where records can be stored

◎◆✳✳✳▼▲

6. using a formula and calculation to determine a record's location

✳◕▲✳✳■✳

7. divisible by only itself and one   ❏❐❋○❋ ■◆○❂❋❏

8. same disk locations for records with different keys   ▲❚❚❏■❚○▲

9. occurs when hashing generates the same location for two records   ❋❏●●❋▲❋❏■

10. parent record at the top of a hierarchical database   ❏❏❏▼ ❏❋❋❏❏❋

11. child record in a network database   ○❋○❂❋❏

12. tables in relational database terminology   ❏❋●❂▼❋❏■▲

13. records (rows) in a relational database   ▼◆❏●❋▲

14. fields in a relational database   ❂▼▼❏❋❂◆▼❋▲

15. range of values an attribute can have in a relational database   ❋❏○❂❋■

16. using a log to automatically reenter transactions in DBMS recovery   ❏❏●●❋❏❏❂❏❋

17. subset of total data created with relational operations   ❖❋❋❩

18. relational operation that picks certain records   ▲❋●❋❋▼

19. relational operation that specifies fields to appear on query output ❏❏❏❋❋❋▼

20. relational operation used to combine two fields   ❋❏❋■

❋❂▼❂❂❂▲❋ ○❏❋❋❂▲ ❋❋○❂■❋ ○❏❏❋ ▲▼❏❏❂❋❋ ▲❏❂❋❋ ▼❋❂■ ❋❂❂▼⬛

❋❋●❋▲ ○❋❋❂◆▲❋ ❏❋ ▼❋❋ ❏❋●❂▼❋❏■▲❋❋❏ ❋❂▼❂⬛ ❩❋❋❋❋ ❋❂■ ○❋

❂▲ ○◆❋❋ ❂▲ ❋❋▼❚ ❏❋❏❋❋■▼ ❏❋ ▼❋❋ ▲▼❏❏❂❋❋ ▲❏❂❋❋✎

SELF TEST ANSWERS

True/False

1. *F* [p. 9.3]
2. *F* [p. 9.6]
3. *T* [p. 9.7]
4. *T* [p. 9.12]
5. *F* [p. 9.13]
6. *F* [p. 9.15]
7. *T* [p. 9.20]
8. *T* [p. 9.23]
9. *T* [p. 9.25]
10. *F* [p. 9.25]

Matching

1. *a* [p. 9.5]
2. *e* [p. 9.6]
3. *c* [p. 9.7]
4. *o* [p. 9.12]
5. *f* [p. 9.12]
6. *h* [p. 9.15]
7. *n* [p. 9.16]
8. *b* [p. 9.17]
9. *j* [p. 9.18]
10. *l* [p. 9.20]

Multiple Choice

1. *d* [p. 9.3]
2. *c* [p. 9.6]
3. *b* [p. 9.6]
4. *a* [p. 9.9]
5. *a* [p. 9.14]
6. *c* [p. 9.17]
7. *a* [p. 9.21]
8. *d* [p. 9.24]
9. *a* [p. 9.25]
10. *b* [p. 9.25]

Fill in the Blanks

1. *data management* [p. 9.2]
2. *deleting* [p. 9.3]
3. *file* [p. 9.4]
4. *Sequential* [p. 9.6]
5. *index* [p. 9.6]
6. *database* [p. 9.12]
7. *hierarchical database* [p. 9.15]
8. *owner* [p. 9.16]
9. *relational operations* [p. 9.21]
10. *database administrator (DBA)* [p. 9.23]

Complete the Table [p. 9.19]

FEATURE	DESCRIPTION
Data Dictionary	*Defines data files and fields*
Utility Program	Creates files and dictionaries, monitors performance, copies data, and deletes unwanted records
Security	*Controls different levels of access to a database*
Replication	Distributes data to other computers
Recovery	*Helps restore database after an equipment or software malfunction*
Query Language	Creates views and specifies report content and format

Puzzle Answer

1. includes procedures for adding, changing, and deleting data

updating
◆□❋♦▼❋■ ❋

2. collection of related data or information stored under a single name

file
❋❋●❋

3. structured groups of related facts

records
□❋❋□□❋▲

4. individual facts that make up records

fields
❋❋❋●❋▲

5. location in a direct file where records can be stored

buckets
♦◆❋❋❋▼▲

6. using a formula and calculation to determine a record's location

hashing
❋♦▲❋❋■❋

7. divisible by only itself and one

prime number
□□❋○❋ ■◆○♦❋□

8. same disk locations for records with different keys

synonyms
▲■◼□◼○▲

9. occurs when hashing generates the same location for two records

collision
❋□●●❋▲❋□■

10. parent record at the top of a hierarchical database

root record
□□□▼ □❋❋□□❋

11. child record in a network database

member
○❋○♦❋□

12. tables in relational database terminology

relations
□❋●♦▼❋□■▲

13. records (rows) in a relational database

tuples
▼◆□●❋▲

14. fields in a relational database

attributes
♦▼▼□❋♦◆▼❋▲

15. range of values an attribute can have in a relational database

domain
❋□○♦❋■

16. using a log to automatically reenter transactions in DBMS recovery

rollforward
□□●●❋□□❒♦□❋

17. subset of total data created with relational operations

view
❖❋❋❒

(continued)

select
_____

18. relational operation that picks certain records

▲✳●✳✳▼

project
_____

19. relational operation that specifies fields to appear on query output

▢▢▢✳✳✳▼

join
_____

20. relational operation used to combine two fields

✳▢✳■

Database models demand more storage space than flat
_____

✳♦▼♦♦♦▲✳ ○▢✳✳●▲ ✳✳○♦■✳ ○▢▢✳ ▲▼▢▢♦✳✳ ▲▢♦✳✳ ▼✳♦■ ✳●♦▼

files because of the relationship data, which can be
_____

✳✳●✳▲ ○✳✳♦♦▲✳ ▢✳ ▼✳✳ ▢✳●♦▼✳▢■▲✳✳▢ ✳♦▼♦⬚ ▶✳✳✳ ✳♦■ ○✳

as much as fifty percent of the storage space.
_____

♦▲ ○♦✳✳ ♦▲ ✳✳✳▼▮ ▢✳▢✳✳■▼ ▢✳ ▼✳✳ ▲▼▢▢♦✳✳ ▲▢♦✳✳✎

CHAPTER 10
Information Systems

CHAPTER OVERVIEW

This chapter examines information systems and the ways they are used in an organization. You discover why information is important to an organization and how managers use information. The management levels in an organization are described, the qualities of information are listed, and the types of information systems are explained. Finally, you learn about integrated information systems and the increasingly significant role played by personal computers in information systems.

CHAPTER OBJECTIVES

After completing this chapter, you will be able to:

• Define the term information system and identify the six elements of an information system

• Describe why information is important to an organization

• Explain how managers use information by describing the four managerial tasks

• Discuss the different levels in an organization and how the information requirements differ for each level

• Describe the different functional areas found in an organization

• Explain the qualities that all information should have

• Describe the different types of information systems and the trend toward integration

• Explain how personal computers are used in management information systems

CHAPTER OUTLINE

I. Why is information important to an organization? [p. 10.2]

Having accurate information on products, _____

_____

An organization's information has both _____

Companies are willing to make the investment in information technology because _____

_____

(continued)

An information strategy _____

Several factors contribute to the need for timely and accurate information:

Expanded markets _____

_____

Increased competition _____

_____

Shorter product life cycles _____

_____

Government regulation _____

_____

Increased cost pressure _____

_____

II. How do managers use information? [p. 10.4]

Managers of an organization are _____

_____

Management tasks:

1. _____

2. _____

3. _____

4. _____

Actual performance is measured against _____

The four tasks are related _____

III. Management levels in an organization [p. 10.5]

Usually classified into three levels, shown above a fourth level consisting of _____

_____

A. Senior management —strategic decisions [p. 10.6]

Senior management (executive or top management) includes the highest management positions in an

organization.

The highest senior management position is _____

The CEO is _____

_____

_____

Senior management primarily is responsible for strategic decisions that _____

_____

The time frame for decisions usually is _____

_____

Senior management decisions often require _____

_____

Problems faced by senior management _____

Lower levels of management tend _____

Senior management also is responsible for _____

_____

Types of reports senior management uses are _____

_____

Senior management supervises middle management

B. Middle management —tactical decisions [p. 10.7]

Middle management is responsible for _____

Makes tactical decisions that _____

_____

Relies on information _____

Types of reports middle management uses are _____

Middle management supervises operational management

C. Operational management —operational decisions [p. 10.7]

Operational management supervises _____

_____

Makes operational decisions that _____

_____

Types of reports used by operational managers are _____

Uses summary and exception reports because _____

_____

D. Nonmanagement employees —on-the-job decisions [p. 10.7]

Nonmanagement employees _____

_____

Type of reports used by nonmanagement _____

_____

More information provided to nonmanagement employees as they are given the responsibility to make
decisions previously made by managers only.

IV. Functional areas in an organization [p. 10.8]

Most organizations are divided into functional areas managed by a senior level manager, such as a vice president

- _____

- _____

- _____

- _____

- _____

A. Other approaches to management organization [p. 10.10]

The process of following the chain of command means _____

_____

(continued)

To improve communication, increase productivity, and decrease the amount of time _____

_____

Common features:

- _____

  _____

- _____

  _____

- _____

  _____

- _____

  _____

Information systems managers have been encouraged _____

_____

Rightsize means _____

In a process called outsourcing _____

Information architecture refers _____

V.   Qualities of valuable information [p. 10.11]

Qualities (characteristics) that information should have:

- _____

- _____

- _____

- _____

- _____

- _____

- _____

VI. Types of information systems [p. 10.13]

Information systems generally are classified into five categories: _____,

_____, _____, _____, and

_____.

A.   Office systems [p. 10.13]

Office systems include software applications for administrative tasks that occur throughout the organization.
Sometimes referred to as productivity software, which includes _____

_____

B.   Transaction processing systems [p. 10.13]

Transaction processing systems (TPS) process _____

_____

_____

In batch processing, _____

With online transaction processing (OLTP), _____

C. Management information systems [p. 10.14]

_____

_____

_____

Executive information systems (EIS) _____

_____

EIS originally were designed _____

_____

Because executives focus on strategic issues, EIS often _____

_____

EIS are difficult to implement because _____

D. Decision support systems [p. 10.16]

Decision support systems (DSS) are _____

_____

Some decision support systems include _____

_____

Online analytical processing (OLAP) systems are _____

_____

DSS sometimes are combined with executive information systems (EIS).

E. Expert systems [p. 10.17]

Expert systems (knowledge systems) _____

_____

Made up of the combined subject knowledge of the human experts, and _____

_____

Although they may appear to think, _____

_____

Primarily are used by _____

_____

Artificial intelligence (AI) is _____

_____

VII. Integrated information systems [p. 10.18]

Although expert systems still operate primarily as separate systems, the trend is clear: _____

_____

VIII. The role of personal computers in information systems [p. 10.19]

Reasons the PC is playing a significant role in modern information systems: _____

_____

_____

(continued)

Many professionals believe that the ideal information system involves _____

_____

_____

IX.   Summary of information systems [p. 10.19]

_____

_____

_____

TERMS

accurate [p. 10.11]

agent software [p. 10.18]

artificial intelligence (AI)
    [p. 10.18]

batch processing [p. 10.14]

board of directors [p. 10.6]

chief executive officer (CEO)
    [p. 10.6]

controlling [p. 10.4]

cost-effective [p. 10.12]

decision support systems (DSS)
    [p. 10.16]

directing [p. 10.4]

downsize [p. 10.11]

executive information system
    (EIS) [p. 10.15]

expert systems [p. 10.17]

finance [p. 10.8]

human resources [p. 10.9]

inference rules [p. 10.17]

information architecture
    [p. 10.11]

information system [p. 10.1, 10.6,
    10.9]

knowledge base [p. 10.17]

knowledge system [p. 10.17]

leading [p. 10.4]

management information system
    (MIS) [p. 10.14]

managers [p. 10.4]

meaningful [p. 10.12]

middle management [p. 10.7]

model [p. 10.16]

nonmanagement employees
    [p. 10.7]

office systems [p. 10.13]

online analytical processing
    (OLAP) systems [p. 10.16]

online transaction processing
    (OLTP) [p. 10.14]

operational decisions [p. 10.7]

operational management
    [p. 10.7]

operations [p. 10.8]

organized [p. 10.12]

organizing [p. 10.4]

outsourcing [p. 10.11]

planning [p. 10.4]

rightsize [p. 10.11]

sales and marketing [p. 10.8]

senior management [p. 10.6]

strategic decisions [p. 10.6]

structured problems [p. 10.6]

tactical decisions [p. 10.7]

timely [p. 10.12]

transaction processing systems
    (TPS) [p. 10.13]

unstructured problems [p. 10.6]

useful [p. 10.12]

verifiable [p. 10.12]

SELF TEST
True/False

_____   1.   Unlike more tangible assets such as buildings and equipment, an organization's information assets have no
             present or future value and no costs associated with their acquisition, maintenance, or storage.

_____   2.   The employee database, once used almost exclusively for payroll purposes, now has been expanded to
             include information companies can use to document their compliance with government regulations and
             guidelines.

_____   3.   Lower-level management plans by preparing a three- to five-year plan that includes strategies on how to
             enter new markets or increase existing market share.

_____   4.   The decision time frame of operational managers usually is very short, such as a day, a week, or a month.

_____   5.   With fewer levels of management, managers are required to rely more on exception reports to help them
             allocate their limited time to the most important areas.

_____   6.   The same information is meaningful to every individual and group within an organization.

_____ 7. In batch processing, transactions are processed as they are entered.

_____ 8. Although expert systems can be used at any level in an organization, to date they primarily have been used by senior management for strategic decisions.

_____ 9. Although expert systems still operate primarily as separate systems, the trend is clear: combine all of an organization's information needs into a single, integrated information system.

_____ 10. One study estimated that the cost to process a million transactions on a personal computer is fifty times more expensive than on a mainframe.

Matching

1. _____ planning

2. _____ organizing

3. _____ leading

4. _____ controlling

5. _____ verifiable

6. _____ timely

7. _____ organized

8. _____ meaningful

9. _____ useful

10. _____ cost-effective

a. management task that involves measuring performance and taking corrective action

b. indicates the information is relevant to the person who receives it

c. management task that consists of obtaining current information on competing companies

d. management task that involves establishing goals and objectives

e. the user can confirm the information, if necessary

f. the information should result in an action being taken or not being taken

g. companies have less time to use information to perfect a product

h. management task that includes identifying and bringing together necessary resources

i. the age of the information is suited to the user of the information

j. the information is correct

k. management task that involves businesses selling their products in as many markets as possible

l. management task that involves instructing and authorizing individuals to perform necessary work

m. the information should be arranged to suit users' requirements

n. the price of the information is less than its value

o. information must comply with government regulations

Multiple Choice

_____ 1. What is an information system?

    a. a systematic inventory of the essential qualities that all information should have

    b. a collection of elements that provides accurate, timely, and useful information

    c. the hierarchy through which information is disseminated around an organization

    d. the transmission of data and information over a communications channel

(continued)

_____ 2. Because companies have less time to perfect a product, they must have accurate information about what customers want before the product is introduced. Which of the following factors has contributed most to this increased need for timely and accurate information?

    a. expanded markets

    b. increased competition

    c. shorter product life cycles

    d. government regulation

_____ 3. Establishing the management structure of an organization, such as the departments and reporting relationships, is part of what management task?

    a. planning

    b. organizing

    c. leading

    d. controlling

_____ 4. Decisions on whether or not to add or discontinue a product line or whether to diversify into a new business are examples of what type of decisions?

    a. strategic

    b. tactical

    c. operational

    d. on-the-job

_____ 5. What level in an organization primarily is responsible for implementing the strategic decisions of executive or top management?

    a. senior management

    b. middle management

    c. operational management

    d. nonmanagement employees

_____ 6. What is a common feature in new approaches to management organization?

    a. more levels of management

    b. employees organized by function, not process

    c. self-managed teams are used wherever possible

    d. all of the above

_____ 7. A sales manager who assigns territories on a geographic basis would need prospect lists sorted by postal code and not by prospect name. This is an example of what quality of information?

    a. accurate

    b. verifiable

    c. timely

    d. organized

_____ 8. What is a transaction processing system (TPS)?

    a. an information system that processes data generated by the day-to-day dealings of an organization

    b. an information system that generates timely and accurate information for managing an organization

    c. an information system designed to help someone reach a decision by summarizing and comparing data from either or both internal and external sources

    d. an information system that combines the knowledge on a given subject of one or more human experts into a computerized system

_____ 9. A vice president of finance wants to know the net effect on company profits if interest rates on borrowed money increase and raw material prices decrease. What type of information systems has been developed to provide this information?
   a. management information systems
   b. executive information systems
   c. decision support systems
   d. expert systems

_____ 10. Which of the following is *not* a reason why the personal computer is playing an increasingly significant role in modern information systems?
   a. as organizations move toward decentralized decision making, PCs have given managers access to the information they need
   b. nonmanagement employees benefit from having information available through networked PCs on their desks or in the production line
   c. for many applications, PCs are more cost effective than larger systems and provide greater flexibility
   d. many professionals believe the ideal information system involves decentralized data stored on multiple PCs and centralized computing by an attached minicomputer or mainframe

Fill in the Blanks

1. All _____ that are implemented on a computer are comprised of six elements: hardware, software, accurate data, trained information systems personnel, knowledgeable users, and documented procedures.

2. _____, one of the factors that has contributed to the increased need for timely and accurate information, means that rival companies are stronger financially and better organized.

3. All _____ perform the tasks of planning, organizing, leading, and controlling, but their area of focus and the information they need is influenced by their level in the organization.

4. _____ is concerned with the long-range direction of an organization.

5. _____, which could include how to best advertise and promote a company's products, are decisions that implement specific programs and plans necessary to accomplish the stated objectives.

6. _____ directly supervise the production and support of an organization's product line; thus, they need detailed information telling what was produced.

7. Although it may seem obvious, the first quality of information is that it should be _____; incorrect information often is worse than no information at all.

8. Some examples of _____ are billing systems, inventory control systems, accounts payable systems, and order entry systems.

9. _____ often include query languages, statistical analysis capabilities, spreadsheets, and graphics to help the user evaluate the data used to reach a conclusion.

10. _____ are computerized systems that simulate the human experts' reasoning and decision-making processes.

Complete the Table

The four management tasks:

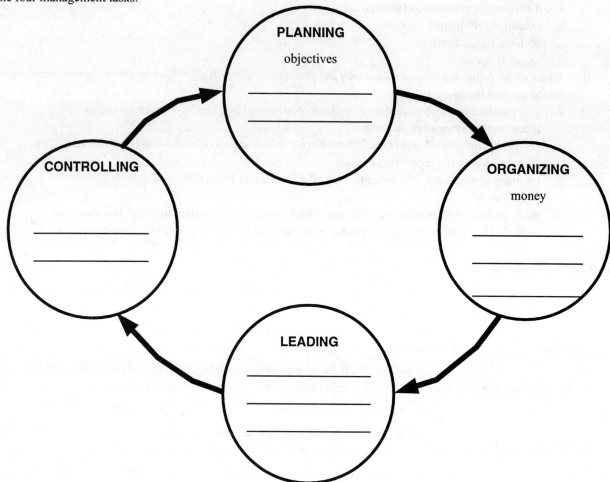

Things to Think About

1. How could a change in one management task affect one or more of the other tasks?

2. Why must a company's information architecture match its organization architecture?

3. How can inaccurate information be worse than no information at all? Why does accurate data not guarantee accurate information?

4. Why does centralized data and decentralized computing allow users and organizations the most flexibility over controlling their information resources?

Puzzle

All of the words described below appear in the puzzle. Words either may be forward or backward, across, up and down, or diagonal. Circle each word as you find it.

```
N  O  I  T  A  M  R  O  F  N  I  S
L  A  G  E  N  T  V  D  S  S  R  T
A  ▢  D  O  W  N  S  I  Z  E  C  R
N  O  N  L  I  N  E  ▢  G  N  O  A
O  T  A  C  T  I  C  A  L  I  R  T
I  N  F  E  R  E  N  C  E  O  E  E
T  P  S  ▢  B  A  T  C  H  R  M  G
A  S  I  E  M  I  D  D  L  E  O  I
R  E  G  D  E  L  W  O  N  K  D  C
E  X  P  E  R  T  S  Y  S  T  E  M
P  B  O  J  E  H  T  N  O  ▢  L  I
O  U  T  S  O  U  R  C  I  N  G  S
```

the men and women responsible for directing the use of an organization's resources

level of management that includes the highest management positions in an organization

decisions that deal with the overall goals and objectives of an organization

level of management responsible for implementing strategic decisions

decisions that implement specific programs and plans to accomplish stated objectives

level of management that supervises production and nonmanagement staff

type of decisions made by nonmanagement employees

move applications away from mainframe and minicomputers to networks of PCs

hiring outside firms to provide information systems support for a contracted fee

should be accurate, verifiable, timely, organized, meaningful, useful, and cost effective

abbreviation for information system that processes data generated by day-to-day transactions

type of processing in which data is collected and processed at a later time

type of transaction processing in which transactions are processed as entered

abbreviation for computer-based system that generates information for managing

abbreviation for management information systems designed for senior management

abbreviation for information systems designed to help someone reach a decision

allows users to ask *what-if* questions by changing one or more variables

combines knowledge on a given subject of one or more human experts

base in an expert system made up of combined subject information of human experts

rules in an expert system that determine how knowledge is used to reach decisions

software that searches Internet for information that matches users' preferences or criteria

SELF TEST ANSWERS

True/False
1. *F* [p. 10.2]
2. *T* [p. 10.3]
3. *F* [p. 10.4]
4. *T* [p. 10.7]
5. *T* [p. 10.11]
6. *F* [p. 10.12]
7. *F* [p. 10.14]
8. *F* [p. 10.18]
9. *T* [p. 10.18]
10. *F* [p. 10.18]

Matching
1. *d* [p. 10.4]
2. *h* [p. 10.4]
3. *l* [p. 10.4]
4. *a* [p. 10.4]
5. *e* [p. 10.12]
6. *i* [p. 10.12]
7. *m* [p. 10.12]
8. *b* [p. 10.12]
9. *f* [p. 10.12]
10. *n* [p. 10.12]

Multiple Choice
1. *b* [p. 10.1]
2. *c* [p. 10.3]
3. *b* [p. 10.4]
4. *a* [p. 10.6]
5. *b* [p. 10.7]
6. *c* [p. 10.10]
7. *d* [p. 10.12]
8. *a* [p. 10.13]
9. *c* [p. 10.16]
10. *d* [p. 10.19]

Fill in the Blanks
1. *information systems* [p. 10.1]
2. *Increased competition* [p. 10.3]
3. *managers* [p. 10.4]
4. *Senior management* [p. 10.6]
5. *Tactical decisions* [p. 10.7]
6. *Operational managers* [p. 10.7]
7. *accurate* [p. 10.11]
8. *transaction processing systems (TPS)* [p. 10.13]
9. *Decision support systems (DSS)* [p. 10.16]
10. *Expert systems* [p. 10.17]

Complete the Table [p. 10.5]

The four management tasks:

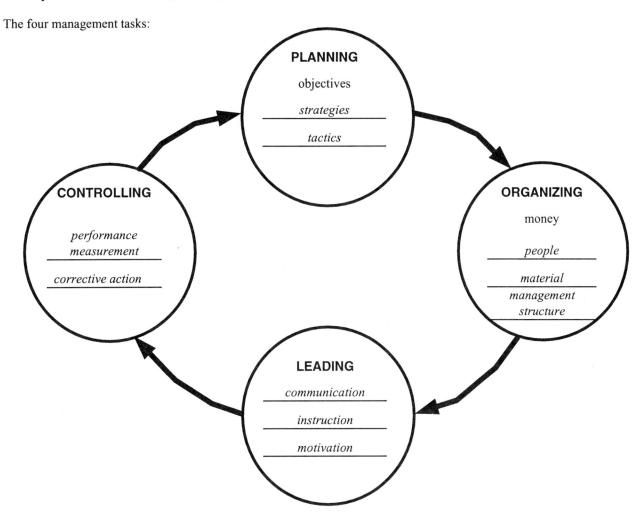

Puzzle Answer

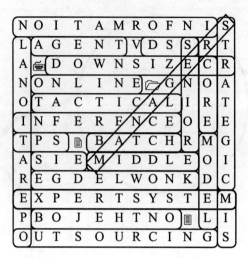

CHAPTER 11
Information Systems Development

CHAPTER OVERVIEW

This chapter examines creating an information system, which is a process known as the system development life cycle. The system development life cycle (SDLC) is defined and ongoing activities performed throughout the cycle: project management, feasibility assessment, documentation, and data and information gathering are explained. You learn what takes place during the system development life cycle's five phases: planning, analysis, design, implementation, and support. To illustrate each phase of the process, a case study about consolidating the monthly statement for the customers of the North Harbor State Bank Company is presented.

CHAPTER OBJECTIVES

After completing this chapter, you will be able to:

- Explain the phases in the system development life cycle
- Identify the guidelines for system development
- Discuss the importance of project management, feasibility assessment, data and information gathering techniques, and documentation
- Identify items that initiate the system development life cycle
- Describe how structured tools, such as entity-relationship diagrams and data flow diagrams, are used in the analysis and design phases
- Discuss the importance of the project dictionary
- Differentiate between commercial application software and custom software
- Identify program development as part of the system development life cycle
- Discuss several techniques used to convert to a new system
- Describe methods used to support an information system

CHAPTER OUTLINE

I. What is the system development life cycle? [p. 11.2]

The system development life cycle (SDLC) is _____

_____

(continued)

The many activities of the SDLC are grouped _____

_____

A. Phases in the system development life cycle [p. 11.2]

    Phases of the SDLC:

      1. _____

      2. _____

      3. _____

      4. _____

      5. _____

B. Guidelines for systems development [p. 11.3]

    The development of an information system should follow three general guidelines:

    (1) _____, (2) _____, and (3) _____

    Using a phased approach involves _____

    _____

    Users include anyone for whom the system _____

    _____

    Having standards helps _____

    _____

C. Who participates in the system development life cycle? [p. 11.3]

    Any person who will be affected by the proposed system should participate.

    Participants can be categorized as _____

    For each system development project, _____

D. Project management [p. 11.4]

    Process of planning, scheduling, and then controlling _____

    _____

    To effectively plan and schedule a project, the project leader must identify these items:

      • _____

      • _____

      • _____

      • _____

      • _____

      • _____

    A project plan _____

    A Gantt chart _____

    A deliverable is _____

    _____

    A popular project management software is _____

E. Feasibility assessment [p. 11.5]

    Is a measure of _____

An ongoing part of the entire development process.

Tested against three criteria:

Operational feasibility measures _____

Technical feasibility measures _____

Economic (cost/benefit) feasibility measures _____

F. Documentation [p. 11.6]

An ongoing part of the entire development process.

Refers to _____

_____

The project notebook stores _____

An automated project notebook is _____

G. Data and information gathering techniques [p. 11.7]

Several methods are used during the system development process to gather data and information:
(1) _____, (2) _____, (3) _____, and
(4) _____

The most important data and information gathering technique is _____

_____

Unstructured interviews rely _____

Structured interviews rely _____

Alternatives to interviews are _____

_____

II. What initiates the system development life cycle? [p. 11.7]

New or modified information systems may be requested for a variety of reasons.

An external reason _____

Change in information requirements

Most obvious reason is _____

A. North Harbor State Bank – a case study [p. 11.9]

_____

_____

_____

III. Planning phase [p. 11.9]

Begins when _____

The steering committee _____

_____

Planning phase involves four major activities: (1) _____,
(2) _____, (3) _____, and (4) _____

Requirements imposed by management or other governing body are given highest priority.

(continued)

A. Planning at North Harbor State Bank [p. 11.10]

_____

_____

_____

IV. Analysis phase [p. 11.11]

Divided into two major tasks: _____

Feasibility study contains one activity: _____

Detailed analysis contains three activities: _____, _____, and

_____

A. The feasibility study [p. 11.11]

Also called _____

Purpose is _____

Most important aspect is _____

Preliminary investigation begins with _____

Upon completion of the preliminary investigation, _____

_____

The feasibility study report contains the following sections:

Introduction _____

Existing system _____

Benefits of a new system _____

Feasibility of a new system _____

Recommendation _____

B. Feasibility study at North Harbor State Bank [p. 11.12]

_____

_____

C. Detailed analysis [p. 11.12]

Involves three major activities: (1) _____

_____ ,

(2) _____ ,

and (3) _____

Detailed analysis sometimes is called _____

_____

Important benefit gained is the building _____

D. Structured analysis and design tools [p. 11.13]

Findings and reports must be written in a manner that is understandable to many different types of readers.

1. Entity-relationship diagrams [p. 11.14]

Each object about which data is stored, is called an entity.

An entity-relationship diagram (ERD) is _____

_____

2. Data flow diagrams [p. 11.15]

    A data flow diagram (DFD) _____

    _____

    A data flow _____

    A process _____

    A data store _____

    A source _____

    A context diagram _____

3. Project dictionary [p. 11.16]

    Also called _____

    The project dictionary _____

    _____

4. Structured English [p. 11.16]

    Process specifications _____

    Structured English _____

5. Decision tables and decision trees [p. 11.17]

    A decision table or decision tree _____

    _____

6. Data dictionary [p. 11.18]

    The data dictionary _____

    _____

    Validation rules _____

E. The build-or-buy decision [p. 11.19]

    After studying the current system and determining all user requirements, the analyst prepares the system

    proposal which _____

    The build-or-buy decision _____

    _____

F. What is commercial application software? [p. 11.19]

    Commercial application software is _____

    _____

    Horizontal application software is _____

    Vertical application software is _____

    Trade publications are _____

G. What is custom software? [p. 11.20]

    It is _____

    The main advantage is _____

    The main disadvantages are _____

(continued)

H.   Detailed analysis at North Harbor State Bank [p. 11.20]

_____

_____

_____

V.   Design phase [p. 11.21]

Consists of two major activities: (1) _____, and
(2) _____

A.   Acquiring essential hardware and software [p. 11.21]

Has four tasks: (1) _____,
(2) _____, (3) _____, and
(4) _____

B.   Identifying technical specifications [p. 11.21]

A request for quotation (RFQ) is _____

A request for proposal (RFP) is _____

A request for information (RFI) is _____

C.   Soliciting vendor proposals [p. 11.22]

You can search for vendors on _____

A value-added reseller (VAR) _____

The advantage of a VAR _____

Another way to find suppliers is _____

D.   Testing and evaluating vendor proposals [p. 11.23]

A popular technique is _____

A benchmark test measures _____

E.   Making a decision [p. 11.24]

When you purchase hardware, you usually own it.

A software license _____

_____

F.   Software acquisition at North Harbor State Bank [p. 11.24]

_____

_____

G.   Detailed design [p. 11.25]

The detailed design sometimes is called _____

1.   Database design [p. 11.25]

Data is the central resource in an information system.

Table structure definitions _____

_____

User access rights _____

2.   Input and output design [p. 11.26]

It is crucial to involve users during input and output design.

Start with output design first _____

A mockup is _____

A layout chart is _____

_____

3. Program design [p. 11.27]

Analyst identifies _____

Program specification package _____

_____

A system flowchart _____

_____

H. Prototyping [p. 11.27]

Rapid application development (RAD) is _____

A prototype is _____

The main advantage _____

A common pitfall _____

I. CASE tools [p. 11.28]

CASE is _____

CASE (or I-CASE) products:

- _____
- _____
- _____
- _____
- _____
- _____

J. Quality review techniques [p. 11.29]

Structured walkthrough _____

The purpose of a walkthrough _____

K. Detailed design at North Harbor State Bank [p. 11.29]

_____

_____

VI. Implementation phase [p. 11.30]

The purpose of implementation is _____

Activities include: (1) _____, (2) _____,

(3) _____, and (4) _____

A. Develop programs [p. 11.30]

Program development life cycle is _____

Steps in program development life cycle: (1) _____,

(2) _____, (3) _____, (4) _____,

(5) _____, and (6) _____

(continued)

B. Install and test the new system [p. 11.30]

_____

Three types of tests:

• System Test   — _____

• _____ — _____

• _____ — _____

C. Train and educate users [p. 11.30]

Training involves _____

Education is the process _____

D. Convert to the new system [p. 11.31]

Involves _____

Methods of conversion:

Direct conversion _____

_____

The advantage _____

The disadvantage_____

Parallel conversion _____

_____

The advantage _____

The disadvantage _____

Phased conversion _____

_____

Pilot conversion _____

_____

Data conversion is _____

E. Implementation at North Harbor State Bank [p. 11.32]

_____

_____

VII. Support phase [p. 11.33]

The purpose is _____

_____

Four major activities: (1) _____, (2) _____,

(3) _____, and (4) _____

Post-implementation system review is _____

Errors are caused from _____

_____

System enhancement involves _____

The purpose of performance monitoring _____

_____

A. Support at North Harbor State Bank [p. 11.33]

VIII. Summary of the system development life cycle [p. 11. 33]

TERMS

acceptance test [p. 11.30]

analysis phase [p. 11.11]

benchmark test [p. 11.24]

build-or-buy decision [p. 11.19]

commercial application software
[p. 11.19]

computer-aided software
engineering (CASE)
[p. 11.28]

context diagram [p. 11.15]

custom software [p. 11.15]

data conversion [p. 11.32]

data dictionary [p. 11.18]

data flow [p. 11.15]

data flow diagram (DFD)
[p. 11.15]

data store [p. 11.15]

decision tables [p. 11.17]

decision trees [p. 11.17]

deliverable [p. 11.5]

design phase [p. 11.21]

desktop video classroom
[p. 11.35]

detailed analysis [p. 11.12]

detailed design specifications
[p. 11.25]

direct conversion [p. 11.31]

distance learning [p. 11.36]

documentation [p. 11.6]

economic feasibility [p. 11.5]

entity [p. 11.14]

entity-relationship diagram (ERD)
[p. 11.14]

feasibility [p. 11.5]

feasibility study [p. 11.11]

Gantt chart [p. 11.4]

horizontal application software
[p. 11.19]

implementation phase [p. 11.30]

integration test [p. 11.30]

JAD session [p. 11.7]

layout chart [p. 11.26]

logic [p. 11.27]

logical design [p. 11.12]

methodology [p. 11.34]

mockup [p. 11.26]

operational feasibility [p. 11.5]

parallel conversion [p. 11.32]

phased conversion [p. 11.32]

phases [p. 11.2]

physical design [p. 11.25]

pilot conversion [p. 11.32]

planning phase [p. 11.9]

post-implementation system
review [p. 11.33]

preliminary investigation
[p. 11.11]

process [p. 11.15]

program development life cycle
(PDLC) [p. 11.30]

program specification package
[p. 11.27]

project dictionary [p. 11.6, 11.16]

project management [p. 11.4]

project notebook [p. 11.6]

project plan [p. 11.4]

project team [p. 11.4]

prototype [p. 11.27]

rapid application development
(RAD) [p. 11.27]

repository [p. 11.6, 11.16]

request for information (RFI)
[p. 11.22]

request for proposal (RFP)
[p. 11.22]

request for quotation (RFQ)
[p. 11.22]

scope [p. 11.4]

source [p. 11.15]

steering committee [p. 11.9]

STRADIS [p. 11.34]

structured analysis and design
[p. 11.13]

structured English [p. 11.16]

structured interview [p. 11.7]

structured walkthrough
[p. 11.29]

support phase [p. 11.33]

system development life cycle
(SDLC) [p. 11.2]

system flowchart [p. 11.27]

system proposal [p. 11.19]

system test [p. 11.30]

technical feasibility [p. 11.5]

trade publications [p. 11.19]

unstructured interview [p. 11.7]

users [p. 11.3]

validation rules [p. 11.18]

value-added reseller (VAR)
[p. 11.22]

vertical application software
[p. 11.19]

SELF TEST

True/False

_____ 1. The activities of the system development life cycle can be grouped into distinct phases: analysis, planning, program development, implementation, and support.

_____ 2. Project management involves planning, scheduling, and controlling the individual activities that make up the system development life cycle.

_____ 3. Feasibility is a measure of how suitable the development of a system will be to the organization.

_____ 4. Vertical application software packages tend to be more widely available (because they can be used by a greater number of organizations) and less expensive than horizontal application software packages.

_____ 5. When you purchase software, what you actually are purchasing is a software license, which is the right to use the software under certain terms and conditions.

_____ 6. A benchmark test measures the time it takes to process a set number of transactions.

_____ 7. During the design phase, the physical design is transformed into a logical design that identifies the procedures to be automated.

_____ 8. The disadvantage of prototyping is that the user is unable to actually experience the system before it is completed.

_____ 9. During the implementation phase, new hardware is installed and tested.

_____ 10. Performance monitoring is an activity that determines if the new system is inefficient at any point and if the inefficiency is causing a problem.

Matching

1. _____ feasibility

2. _____ economic feasibility

3. _____ data flow diagram (DFD)

4. _____ project dictionary

5. _____ structured English

6. _____ decision tree

7. _____ request for proposal (RFP)

8. _____ request for quotation (RFQ)

9. _____ system flowchart

10. _____ structured walkthrough

a. measures whether the lifetime benefits of a system will exceed the lifetime costs

b. identifies the actions that should be taken under different conditions

c. provides assurance that dollar amounts recorded in accounting records are correct

d. a vendor selects products that meet requirements and submits a price

e. petition for a written price estimate on an item to be purchased

f. specifies what levels of security are required for different processes

g. graphically shows the movement of data through a system

h. contains all the documentation and deliverables associated with a project

i. assures the complete and accurate conversion of data from source documents

j. demonstrates to the users that the system can meet user-designed test criteria

k. a measure of how suitable the development of a system will be to the organization

l. step-by-step review of any deliverable

m. evaluates work completed so far to determine whether to proceed

n. style of writing that describes the steps in a process

o. shows the timing of the processes, outputs generated, database tables required, and types of input devices

Multiple Choice

_____ 1. Which of the following is *not* a phase of the system development life cycle?

    a. analysis

    b. customizing

    c. design

    d. implementation

_____ 2. Which of the following is particularly useful in project management?

    a. a Gantt chart

    b. a CASE workbench

    c. a design review

    d. a benchmark test

_____ 3. What is an excellent way of showing the desired action when the action depends on multiple conditions?

    a. a data flow diagram

    b. a data dictionary

    c. a process specification

    d. a decisions table

_____ 4. What is commercial application software?

    a. already developed software available for purchase

    b. software used by many different types of organizations

    c. software developed for a unique way of doing business

    d. software developed by the user or at the user's request

_____ 5. During which step in the design phase are a request for proposal (RFP) and a request for quotation (RFQ) prepared?

    a. soliciting vendor proposals

    b. identifying technical specifications

    c. acquiring essential software

    d. test and evaluate vendor proposals

_____ 6. What are user access rights?

    a. which data elements a user can access

    b. when they can access the data elements

    c. what actions they can perform on the data elements

    d. all of the above

(continued)

_____ 7. What two types of layouts should be developed for each input and output?

     a. data dictionary and project dictionary

     b. system flowchart and prototype

     c. mockup and layout chart

     d. graphics and narrative

_____ 8. What is the first step in program development?

     a. designing the program

     b. coding the program

     c. testing the program

     d. analyzing the problem

_____ 9. What conversion method consists of continuing to process on the old system while some or all of the data also is processed on the new system?

     a. direct conversion

     b. parallel conversion

     c. phased conversion

     d. pilot conversion

_____ 10. What is the support phase in the SDLC?

     a. the separation of a system into its component parts to determine how it works

     b. the development of programs and acquisition of equipment

     c. the phase when people actually begin to use the new system

     d. the process of providing continuous assistance for the system after it is implemented

Fill in the Blanks

1. _____ is an organized set of activities used to guide those involved through the development of an information system.

2. _____ is the compilation and summarization of data and information, including reports, diagrams, programs, or any other deliverable generated during the project.

3. The purpose of the _____ is to determine whether or not the problem or enhancement identified in a project is worth pursuing.

4. Detailed analysis sometimes is called _____ because you develop the proposed solution without regard to any specific hardware or software.

5. _____ is software used by many different types of organizations, such as accounting packages.

6. The most common reason for developing _____ is that an organization's software requirements are so unique that it is unable to find a package meeting its needs.

7. _____ sell not only software, but also the computer equipment.

8. The detailed design sometimes is called _____ because it specifies hardware and software for automated procedures.

9. Important activities of the _____ phase include developing programs, training and educating users, and converting to the new system.

10. The _____ consists of four major activities: conduct a post-implementation system review, identify errors, identify enhancements, and monitor performance.

Complete the Table

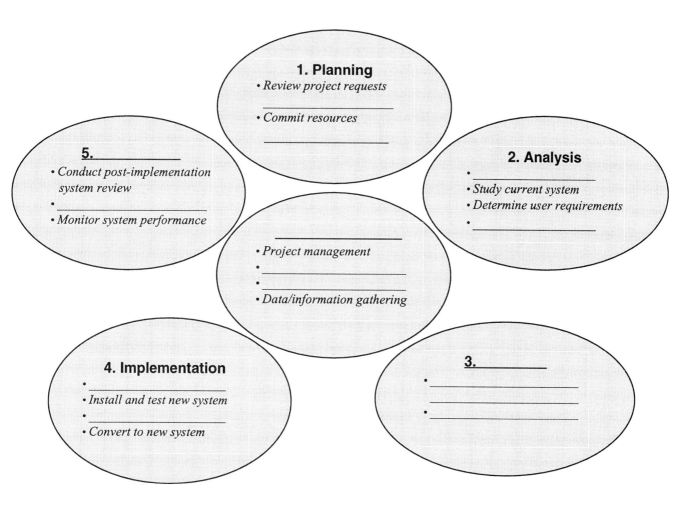

Things to Think About

1. Why does the start of many activities in the system development life cycle depend on the successful completion of other activities?

2. Although it is created in the analysis phase, how could a data dictionary be used in subsequent phases of the system development life cycle?

3. Why would an organization probably have to change some of its methods and procedures to adapt to the way commercial application software functions?

4. How can untrained users prevent the estimated benefits of a new system from ever being obtained or, worse, contribute to less efficiency and more costs than when the old system was operational?

Puzzle

Across

2. a type of interview where the interviewee (user) directs the conversation

6. a computer-based tool designed to support one or more phases of the SDLC

11. a conversion method of running the old and new system side-by-side

12. a type of feasibility that measures whether lifetime benefits will exceed the lifetime costs

13. a type of application software developed by users for specific user needs

14. a document that asks vendors to select products and provide prices

Down

1. a type of rule that includes codes, ranges, or values

3. a document that asks vendors to supply prices for specific products

4. compilation and summarization of data and information

5. a test that measures the time it takes to process a set number of transactions

7. phase in which users are trained and educated

8. a type of application software that can be used by many organizations

9. a tangible item transmitted on time according to plan

Across

15. a tree-shaped tool used to identify action that should be taken under certain conditions

18. a bar chart that represents project phases or activities

20. a working model of a proposed system

22. phase in which project requests are prioritized

23. abbreviation for the five phases of the life cycle

24. a tool used to graphically represent the association between objects

25. a type of application software that is developed for a specific industry

Down

10. type of input or output design that contains actual data

15. a tool used to graphically represent the flow of data in a system

16. a test performed by end-users, checks that the new systems works with actual data

17. phase in which hardware and software are acquired

19. type of design during detailed analysis because it does not focus on specific pieces of hardware or software

21. conversion method of running a new system at only one location

SELF TEST ANSWERS

True/False
1. F [p. 11.2]
2. T [p. 11.4]
3. T [p. 11.5]
4. F [p. 11.19]
5. T [p. 11.24]
6. T [p. 11.24]
7. F [p. 11.25]
8. F [p. 11.27]
9. T [p. 11.30]
10. T [p. 11.33]

Matching
1. k [p. 11.5]
2. a [p. 11.5]
3. g [p. 11.15]
4. h [p. 11.16]
5. n [p. 11.16]
6. b [p. 11.17]
7. d [p. 11.22]
8. e [p. 11.22]
9. o [p. 11.27]
10. l [p. 11.29]

Multiple Choice
1. b [p. 11.2]
2. a [p. 11.4]
3. d [p. 11.17]
4. a [p. 11.19]
5. b [p. 11.22]
6. d [p. 11.25]
7. c [p. 11.26]
8. d [p. 11.30]
9. b [p. 11.32]
10. d [p. 11.33]

Fill in the Blanks
1. System development life cycle (SDLC) [p. 11.2]
2. Documentation [p. 11.6]
3. feasibility study or preliminary investigation [p. 11.11]
4. logical design [p. 11.12]
5. Horizontal application software [p. 11.19]
6. custom software [p. 11.20]
7. Value-added resellers (VARs) [p. 11.22]
8. physical design [p. 11.25]
9. implementation [p. 11.30]
10. support phase [p. 11.33]

Complete the Table [p. 11.2]

1. Planning
- *Review project requests*
- Prioritize project requests
- Commit resources
- Identify project development team

5. Support
- *Conduct post-implementation system review*
- Identify errors and enhancements
- *Monitor system performance*

Ongoing Activities
- *Project management*
- Feasibility assessment
- Documentation
- *Data/information gathering*

2. Analysis
- Conduct feasibility study
- *Study current system*
- *Determine user requirements*
- Recommend solution

4. Implementation
- Develop programs
- *Install and test new system*
- Train and educate users
- *Convert to new system*

3. Design
- Acquire hardware and software, if necessary
- Develop details of system

Puzzle Answer

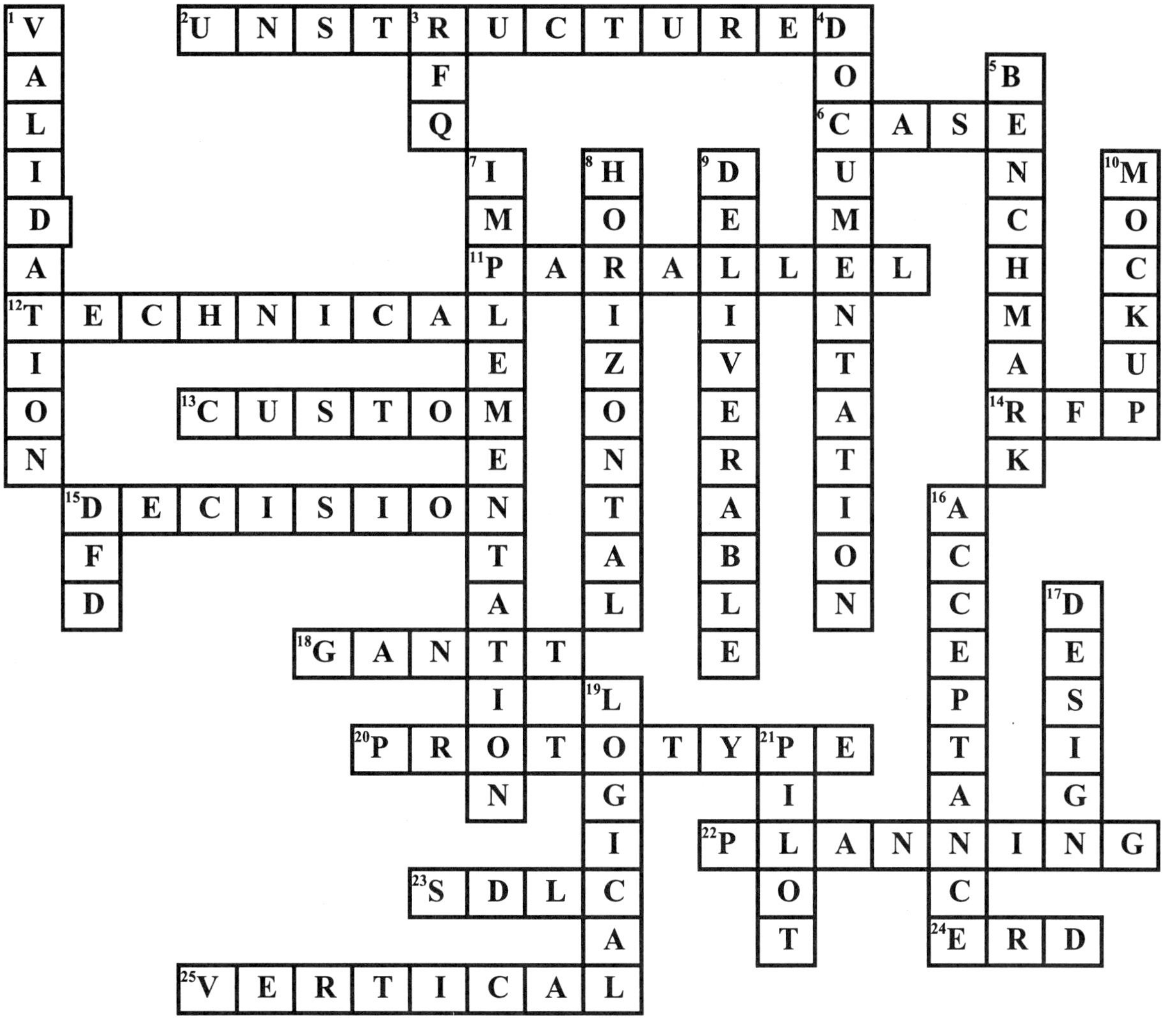

Across / Down solutions (crossword grid):

- 1 Down: VALIDATION
- 2 Across: UNSTRUCTURED
- 3 Down: RFQ / IFMLEMENTATION
- 4 Down: DOCUMENTATION
- 5 Down: BENCHMARK
- 6 Across: CASE
- 7 Down: IMPLEMENTATION
- 8 Down: HORIZONTAL
- 9 Down: DELIVERABLE
- 10 Down: MOCKUP
- 11 Across: PARALLEL
- 12 Across: TECHNICAL
- 13 Across: CUSTOM
- 14 Across: RFP
- 15 Across: DECISION
- 16 Down: ACCEPTANCE
- 17 Down: DESIGN
- 18 Across: GANTT
- 19 Down: LOGICAL
- 20 Across: PROTOTYPE
- 21 Down: PILOT
- 22 Across: PLANNING
- 23 Across: SDLC
- 24 Across: ERD
- 25 Across: VERTICAL

Grid letters as shown:

Row 1: V — U N S T R U C T U R E D — — B
Row: A — F — — O — B
Row: L — Q — — C A S E — N
Row: I — I H D — U — N — M
Row: D — M O E — M — C — O
Row: A — P A R A L L E L — H — C
Row: T E C H N I C A L — I I — N — M — K
Row: I — E Z V — T — A — U
Row: O — C U S T O M O E — — R F P
Row: N — E N R — A — K
Row: D E C I S I O N T A B — I — A
Row: F — T A L — O — C
Row: D — A L — N — C — D
Row: G A N T T — E — E — E
Row: I — L — P — S
Row: P R O T O T Y P E — T — I
Row: N — G — I — A — G
Row: I — P L A N N I N G
Row: S D L C — O — C
Row: A — T — E R D
Row: V E R T I C A L

CHAPTER 12

Program Development and Programming Languages

CHAPTER OVERVIEW

This chapter focuses on the steps taken to write a program, the available tools that make the program development process more efficient, and the different languages used to write programs. Computer program and program development are defined. You examine each of the six steps in program development: (1) analyze problem, (2) design program, (3) code program, (4) test program, (5) formalize solution, and (6) maintain program. Programming language is defined and categories of programming languages are discussed. You learn about programming languages, including object-oriented programming, used today and factors to be considered when choosing a programming language. Program development tools, such as application generators, macros, and rapid application development tools are presented. Finally, scripting languages are discussed.

CHAPTER OBJECTIVES

After completing this chapter, you will be able to:

* Define the term computer program

* Explain the six steps in program development life cycle

* Describe top-down program design

* Explain structured program design and the three basic control structures

* Define the term programming language

* Explain the differences among the categories of programming languages

* Discuss the object-oriented approach to program development

* Identify programming languages commonly used today

* Discuss application generators, macros, and RAD tools

* Discuss how HTML is used to create a Web page

* Identify various uses of a script and popular scripting languages

CHAPTER OUTLINE

I.   What is a computer program? [p. 12.2]

A computer program is _____

_____

A programming language is _____

_____

II. The program development life cycle [p. 12.2]

PDLC is _____

Steps in the program development life cycle:

(1) _____   (4) _____

(2) _____   (5) _____

(3) _____   (6) _____

Program development is an ongoing process within an information system.

A.   What initiates the program development life cycle? [p. 12.3]

Requests for a new or modified program usually occur at the end of the analysis phase of the system development life cycle.

The program specification package _____

_____

A programming team usually _____

III. Step 1 —analyze problem [p. 12.4]

Consists of three major tasks: (1) _____, (2) _____, and (3)

_____

Program specification package contains _____

_____

The programmer meets with the systems analyst and the users to _____

_____

The programmer should never make _____

An IPO chart _____

_____

IV. Step 2 —design program [p. 12.4]

Designing the program consists of three tasks: (1) _____, (2) _____,
and (3) _____

A.   Top-down design [p. 12.5]

The objective of top-down design is _____

_____

The main routine is _____

Subroutines are _____

A module is _____

A hierarchy chart (structure chart, or _____, or _____) is

_____

A benefit to the top-down approach _____

B. Structured design [p. 12.6]

A graphic or written description _____

_____

Structured design is _____

_____

A control structure is _____

1. Sequence control structure [p. 12.6]

In the sequence control structure, _____

_____

2. Selection control structure [p. 12.6]

_____

The selection control structure sometimes is called _____

The case control structure is a _____

3. Repetition control structure [p. 12.7]

Also called _____

_____

Two forms of repetition control structure:

_____ – _____

_____

_____ – _____

_____

C. Proper program design [p. 12.8]

A proper program is _____

_____

Each of its control structures has the following characteristics:

1. No dead code _____

2. No infinite loops _____

3. One entry point _____

4. One exit point _____

D. Design tools [p. 12.9]

Purpose is _____

1. Program flowchart [p. 12.9]

A program flowchart _____

_____

_____ published a set of standards used

to represent various operations performed on a computer.

(continued)

    2.   Nassi-Schneiderman chart [p. 12.10]

    _____

    _____

    3. Pseudocode [p. 12.11]

       In pseudocode, _____

    _____

E.   Quality review techniques [p. 12.12]

Desk checking is _____

Test data is _____

Desk checking involves five steps:

1. _____

2. _____

3. _____

4. _____

5. _____

A logic error occurs when _____

The structured walkthrough is _____

_____

V.   Step 3 —code program [p. 12.13]

Requires two steps: (1) _____

and (2) _____

Syntax is _____

Code standards _____

As you enter the program into the computer, you should take time to document the program code thoroughly.

Global comments are _____

Internal comments _____

VI.   Step 4 —test program [p. 12.13]

Errors uncovered during testing usually are one of two types: (1) _____ or

(2) _____

Syntax errors are _____

The procedure for checking logic errors _____

Test data should include _____

One purpose of test data is to make _____

A bug is _____

Debugging refers to _____

A debug utility, also known as a _____

_____

VII.   Step 5 —formalize solution [p. 12.15]

_____

_____

_____

VIII. Step 6 —maintain program [p. 12.15]

Involves (1) _____ and (2) _____

One type of maintenance occurs when _____

A more common type of maintenance _____

IX. Summary of the program development life cycle [p. 12.16]

The key to developing high-quality programs for an information system is

_____

_____

X. What is a programming language? [p. 12.16]

A programming language is _____

_____

XI. Categories of programming languages [p. 12.16]

Five major categories: _____, _____,

_____, _____, and _____

A low-level language _____

A high-level language _____

A. _____ [p. 12.17]

Is the only language _____

Instructions use _____

Disadvantages include _____

_____

B. Assembly language [p. 12.18]

Written as symbols and codes

Referred to as _____

Advantages include _____

_____

The program containing the assembly language code is called a source program.

An assembler _____

Can include macro instructions, which _____

C. Third-generation languages [p. 12.19]

Three categories: _____, _____, and

_____

A third-generation language (3GL) instruction is _____

Procedural languages are _____

_____

(continued)

Like assembly language programs, the 3GL code is called the source program and must be translated into machine language before the computer can understand it.

A compiler _____

_____

Object code or object program is _____

A compiler checks a program's _____ and

then produces _____

An interpreter _____

_____

_____

Advantage of interpreters: _____

Disadvantage of interpreters: _____

D.   Fourth-generation languages (4GL) [p. 12.20]

Uses _____

Described as a nonprocedural language, meaning _____

_____

Many 4GLs work in conjunction _____

SQL is _____

A report generator, or report writer, _____

_____

The emergence of software and program development tools such as query languages and report writers has empowered users by giving them the ability to process reports on their own.

E.   Natural languages [p. 12.21]

Sometimes called a fifth-generation language, _____

_____

Often are associated with _____

XII.   Object-oriented program development [p. 12.21]

Newer approach to developing software that allows programmers to _____

_____

With the object-oriented approach, _____

The procedures in the object are called _____

Data elements are called _____

Encapsulation is _____

An object may be part of a larger category of objects, called a class.

Each class contains _____

A superclass _____

Inheritance is _____

An object instance _____

A message tells _____

A major benefit of the object-oriented approach is the ability to reuse and modify existing objects.

A.   Object-oriented programming [p. 12.23]

Object-oriented programming (OOP) languages are described as being event-driven, meaning _____

_____

_____

XIII. Popular programming languages [p. 12.23]

Although hundreds of programming languages have been developed, only a few are used widely enough today to be recognized as industry standards.

A.   BASIC [p. 12.23]

_____

_____

_____

B.   Visual Basic [p. 12.24]

_____

_____

_____

C.   COBOL [p. 12.25]

_____

_____

_____

D.   C [p. 12.26]

_____

_____

_____

E.   C++ [p. 12.26]

_____

_____

F.   FORTRAN [p. 12.27]

_____

_____

G.   Pascal [p. 12.27]

_____

_____

H.   Ada [p. 12.28]

_____

_____

_____

(continued)

    I.   RPG [p. 12.28]

_____

_____

    J.   Other programming languages [p. 12.29]

_____

_____

XIV. How to select a programming language [p. 12.29]

    Factors to be considered:

    (1) _____

    (2) _____

    (3) _____

    (4) _____

XV. Program development tools [p. 12.30]

_____

_____

    A.   Application generators [p. 12.30]

        Application generators (program generators) are _____

_____

        Some create _____

        A form builder, or screen painter, _____

_____

        A menu generator _____

_____

    B.   Macros [p. 12.31]

        A series of statements that instructs an application how to complete a task

        Used to _____

        Created by (1) _____ and (2) _____

        A macro recorder _____

        Many applications use Visual Basic as the macro programming language because _____

_____

    C.   RAD tools: Visual Basic, Delphi, and PowerBuilder [p. 12.32]

        Rapid application development (RAD) is _____

        The idea behind prototyping _____

        A component is _____

        1.   Visual Basic [p. 12.33]

_____

_____

        2.   Delphi [p. 12.33]

_____

3. PowerBuilder [p. 12.33]

_____

_____

XVI. HTML [p.12.34]

Authors of Web pages use a language called _____

Although not actually a programming language _____

_____

A stand-alone HTML editor _____

An add-on HTML editor _____

An advantage of an add-on HTML editor is _____

_____

A. Script and scripting languages: Java and PERL [p. 12.36]

A script is _____

Scripts are written for three reasons: (1) _____,

(2) _____, and (3) _____

1. Imagemap [p. 12.36]

_____

_____

2. Counter [p. 12.36]

A script that keeps track of the number of visitors to a Web site

3. Animation [p. 12.36]

Because animation requires a lot of processing overhead, _____

_____

4. Processing form [p. 12.36]

Used to collect data from visitors to a Web site and send to the server for processing

5. Java [p. 12.36]

_____

JavaScript can _____

An applet _____

_____

6. PERL [p. 12.36]

Stands for Practical Extraction and Reporting Language and was originally designed as a procedural language.

XVIII. Summary of program development and programming languages

_____

_____

TERMS

Ada [p. 12.28]
add-on HTML editor [p. 12.35]
applet [p. 12.36]
application generator [p. 12.30]
assembler [p. 12.18]
assembly language [p. 12.18]
attributes [p. 12.21]

BASIC [p. 12.23]
bugs [p. 12.15]

C [p. 12.26]
C++ [p. 12.26]
case control structure [p. 12.7]
class [p. 12.22]
COBOL [p. 12.25]
code standards [p. 12.13]
coding [p. 12.13]
compiler [p. 12.19]
component [p. 12.33]
computer program [p. 12.2]
continuous speech input
    [p. 12.39]
control structure [p. 12.6]
counter [p. 12.36]

dead code [p. 12.8]
debug utility [p. 12.15]
debugger [p. 12.15]
debugging [p. 12.15]
Delphi [p. 12.33]
desk checking [p. 12.12]
discreet speech input [p. 12.39]
do-until control structure
    [p. 12.8]
do-while control structure
    [p. 12.8]

empowered [p. 12.21]
encapsulation [p. 12.22]
entry point [p. 12.9]
event [p. 12.23]
exit point [p. 12.9]

form builder [p. 12.30]
formalizing the solution
    [p. 12.15]
FORTRAN [p. 12.27]
fourth-generation language (4GL)
    [p. 12.20]

hierarchy chart [p. 12.5]

high-level language [p. 12.16]
HyperText Markup Language
    (HTML) [p. 12.34]

if-then-else control structure
    [p. 12.7]
imagemaps [p. 12.36]
infinite loop [p. 12.8]
inheritance [p. 12.22]
interpreter [p. 12.20]
IPO chart [p. 12.4]

Java [p. 12.36]
JavaScript [p. 12.36]

logic error [p. 12.12]
logic errors [p. 12.14]
low-level language [p. 12.16]

machine language [p. 12.17]
machine-dependent [p. 12.17]
machine-independent [p. 12.19]
macro [p. 12.18, 12.31]
maintaining [p. 12.15]
menu generator [p. 12.30]
message [p. 12.22]
methods [p. 12.21]
mnemonics [p. 12.18]
module [p. 12.5]

Nassi-Schneiderman (N-S) chart
    [p. 12.10]
natural language [p. 12.21]
natural speech input [p. 12.39]
nonprocedural language
    [p. 12.20]

object [p. 12.21]
object code [p. 12.19]
object instance [p. 12.22]
object program [p. 12.19]
object-oriented [p. 12.21]
object-oriented programming
    (OOP) language [p. 12.23]
operations [p. 12.21]

Pascal [p. 12.27]
PERL [p. 12.36]
PowerBuilder [p. 12.33]
procedural languages [p. 12.19]
processing form [p. 12.36]
program development life cycle
    (PDLC) [p. 12.2]

program development tools
    [p. 12.30]
program flowchart [p. 12.9]
program generator [p. 12.30]
program logic [p. 12.6]
program specification package
    [p. 12.3]
programming language [p. 12.2,
    12.16]
programming team [p. 12.3]
proper program [p. 12.8]
prototyping [p. 12.32]
pseudocode [p. 12.11]

query language [p. 12.20]

rapid application development
    (RAD) [p. 12.32]
record a macro [p. 12.31]
repetition control structure
    [p. 12.7]
report generator [p. 12.21]
report writer [p. 12.21]
RPG [p. 12.28]

screen painter [p. 12.30]
script [p. 12.36]
selection control structure
    [p. 12.6]
sequence control structure
    [p. 12.6]
solution algorithm [p. 12.6]
source program [p. 12.18]
standalone HTML editor
    [p. 12.35]
structured design [p. 12.6]
structured walkthrough [p. 12.12]
subclasses [p. 12.22]
superclass [p. 12.22]
symbolic addresses [p. 12.18]
symbolic instruction codes
    [p. 12.18]
symbolic programming language
    [p. 12.18]
syntax [p. 12.13]
syntax error [p. 12.14]

test [p. 12.13]
test data [p. 12.12]
third-generation language (3GL)
    [p. 12.19]

top-down design [p. 12.5]

variables [p. 12.21]

Visual Basic [p. 12.24, 12.33]

voice-aware [p. 12.39]

SELF TEST
True/False

_____ 1. A computer program is a detailed set of instructions that directs a computer to perform the tasks necessary to process data into information.

_____ 2. The program specification package communicates the input, output, processing, and data requirements of each program to the programmer.

_____ 3. Structured design is a methodology in which all program logic is constructed from a combination of three control structures or constructs.

_____ 4. The first control structure, called the sequence control structure, gives programmers a way to represent conditional program logic.

_____ 5. Code standards established by the American National Standards Institute (ANSI) enable the same program to work on different types of computers.

_____ 6. While an interpreter translates an entire program, a compiler translates one program statement at a time and then executes the resulting machine language before translating the next program statement.

_____ 7. Fourth-generation languages are nonprocedural and can be used by individuals with very little programming background.

_____ 8. Object-oriented programming (OOP) is a newer approach to developing software that allows programmers to create objects, a combination of data and programs in a single unit.

_____ 9. Most of the programming languages used extensively enough to be recognized as industry standards are high-level programming languages that can be used on a variety of computers.

_____ 10. If a program is going to work with other existing or future programs, ideally it should be written in a different language than the other programs.

Matching

1. _____ BASIC

2. _____ Visual Basic

3. _____ COBOL

4. _____ C

5. _____ C++

6. _____ FORTRAN

7. _____ Pascal

8. _____ Ada

9. _____ HYPERTALK

10. _____ LISP

a. originally designed as a programming language to write system software

b. developed for teaching structured programming concepts

c. developed by Apple to manipulate cards that can contain text, graphics, and sound

d. low-level programming language written for a specific processor

e. nonprocedural, fourth-generation programming language

f. only programming language that has no rules (syntax) to govern its use

g. its English-like statements make them easy to read, write, and maintain

(continued)

h. designed as a programming language to be used by scientists, engineers, and mathematicians

i. fundamental languages of the computer's processor; written in binary code

j. query language that allows the user to enter a question as if speaking to another person

k. LISt Processing, a language used for artificial intelligence applications

l. designed to be a simple, interactive programming language for college students to learn and use

m. object-oriented version of the C programming language

n. designed to meet the needs of embedded computer systems

o. developed in the early 1990s as an application to assist programmers in developing other event-driven Windows applications

Multiple Choice

_____ 1. What is the process called that programmers follow to create computer programs that are correct (produce accurate information) and maintainable (easy to modify)?
   a. program analysis
   b. program development
   c. program implementation
   d. program maintenance

_____ 2. During which step in the process of program development do programmers write the actual program instructions?
   a. reviewing specifications
   b. designing
   c. coding
   d. testing

_____ 3. Which of the following is *not* one of the three main program design concepts emphasized in top-down design?
   a. main routines
   b. modules
   c. control structures
   d. subroutines

_____ 4. The do-while structure is a form of what control structure?
   a. sequence structure
   b. selection structure
   c. case structure
   d. repetition control structure

_____ 5. What are syntax errors?
   a. violations of the grammar rules of the language in which a program was written
   b. faulty sequences of program instructions that lead to inaccurate results
   c. data outside the normal range designed to break or crash a program
   d. instructions that tell a computer to do something it is incapable of doing

____ 6. What category of programming languages is described as nonprocedural, meaning that the programmer does not specify the procedures to be used to accomplish a task?
    a.   machine languages
    b.   assembly languages
    c.   high-level languages
    d.   fourth-generation languages

____ 7. What characteristics of OOP languages allow them to be described as event-driven?
    a.   encapsulation because details are hidden from the user
    b.   the methods because they direct the operations of the program
    c.   messages because they tell the OOP object exactly what to do
    d.   inheritance because one event is the same as other events

____ 8. What is considered the first high-level programming language developed and is noted for its capability to handle complex mathematical and logical expressions?
    a.   BASIC
    b.   COBOL
    c.   C
    d.   FORTRAN

____ 9. Which is *not* one of the factors to be considered in choosing a programming language?
    a.   the programming standards of the organization
    b.   the need for the application to be portable
    c.   the suitability of the language to the application
    d.   the need for program testing and documentation

____ 10. What does a menu generator do?
    a.   represents all the logical steps of a program by a combination of symbols and text
    b.   writes the logical steps in the solution to a problem as English statements with indentations to represent control structures
    c.   lets the user specify a list of processing options that can be selected
    d.   allows the user to design an input or output screen by entering the names and descriptions of the input and output data

Fill in the Blanks

1. The process of _____ has evolved into a series of six steps: analyze problem, design program, code program, test program, formalize solution, and maintain program.

2. In top-down program design, _____ often are used to decompose and represent the modules of a program.

3. Once the program modules have been identified, each module is broken down into a step-by-step procedure called a(n) _____ .

4. A variation of the selection control structure is the _____ , which is used when a condition being tested can yield one of three or more possibilities.

5. Most programming languages include a(n) _____ that identifies syntax errors and allows the programmer to find logic errors by examining program values while the program runs in slow motion.

6. A(n) _____ is a set of words, symbols, and codes that enables the programmer to communicate the solution algorithm to the computer.

7. A(n) _____ language is machine-dependent; that is, it is written to run on one particular computer.

(continued)

8. A(n) _____ tells the object what to do; that is, it indicates the name of the method to be used.

9. A program that allows an application to be built without writing extensive code in a programming language is called a(n) _____.

10. A(n) _____ is a series of statements that instructs an application how to complete a task.

Complete the Table

ALGOL	ALGOrithmic Language, the first structured procedural language
APL	_____
	_____
_____	Similar to C, used for device control applications
_____	An object-oriented programming language developed by Apple to manipulate cards that can contain text, graphics, and sound
LISP	_____
_____	An educational tool used to teach programming and problem-solving to children
MODULA-2	_____
PILOT	_____
_____	Programming Language One, a business and scientific language that combines many features of FORTRAN and COBOL
PROLOG	_____
SMALLTALK	_____

Things to Think About

1. Why should a programmer not change design specifications without the agreement of the systems analyst and the user?

2. Prior to the introduction of structured program design, programmers designed programs by focusing on the detailed steps required for a program and creating logical solutions for each new combination of conditions as it was encountered. Why did developing programs in this manner lead to poorly designed programs?

3. Why is it better to find errors and make needed changes to a program during the design step than to make them later in the development process?

4. Would it be more difficult to uncover syntax errors or logic errors in a program? Why?

Puzzle

Write the word described by each clue in the puzzle below. Words can be written forward or backward, across, up-and-down, or diagonally. The initial letter of each word already appears in the puzzle.

	P									
B								S		
			A		C					
R		⬛	L	O						
				C		L				
					D		⌨	🖱	S	
	A						T			
E		A				N				
						S				
					C					
			P		C					
A	M					B			D	

type of control structure used when a condition can lead to more than two alternatives

type of control structure that means one or more processes continue to occur as long as a given condition remains true

type of control structure in which the condition is tested at the end of the loop

point where a control structure is started

point where a control structure is left

design tool in which the logical steps in a problem's solution are written as English statements

process of stepping through the logic of the algorithm with test data

type of errors that are violations of grammar rules

type of errors where the expected results and the actual results do not match

type of data that simulates real data the program will process when it is implemented

process of locating and correcting program errors

program error

type of language used to write the instructions that direct a computer to process data into information

program that converts assembly language programs into machine language programs

converts an entire high-level language program into a machine language program

type of program to be converted by a compiler

language that allows a person to enter a question as if talking to another person

generator that lets the user specify a list of processing options that can be selected

generator that allows the user to design an input or output display

in OOP, combinations of data and program instructions

in OOP, objects that are part of larger categories

stands for Beginners All-purpose Symbolic Instruction Code

stands for COmmon Business Oriented Language

programming language named for woman believed to have written the first computer program

the first structured programming language

programming language that uses special symbols to manipulate tables of numbers

programming language introduced to assist business in generating reports

SELF TEST ANSWERS

True/False	Matching	Multiple Choice
1. *T* [p. 12.2]	1. *l* [p. 12.23]	1. *b* [p. 12.2]
2. *T* [p. 12.3]	2. *o* [p. 12.24]	2. *c* [p. 12.2]
3. *T* [p. 12.6]	3. *g* [p. 12.25]	3. *c* [p. 12.5]
4. *F* [p. 12.6]	4. *a* [p. 12.26]	4. *d* [p. 12.7]
5. *T* [p. 12.13]	5. *m* [p. 12.26]	5. *a* [p. 12.14]
6. *F* [p. 12.19]	6. *h* [p. 12.27]	6. *d* [p. 12.20]
7. *T* [p. 12.20]	7. *b* [p. 12.27]	7. *c* [p. 12.23]
8. *T* [p. 12.21]	8. *n* [p. 12.28]	8. *d* [p. 12.27]
9. *T* [p. 12.23]	9. *c* [p. 12.29]	9. *d* [p. 12.29]
10. *F* [p. 12.29]	10. *k* [p. 12.29]	10. *c* [p. 12.30]

Fill in the Blanks

1. *program development* [p. 12.2]
2. *hierarchy charts* [p. 12.5]
3. *solution algorithm* [p. 12.6]
4. *case control structure* [p. 12.7]
5. *debugger* [p. 12.15]
6. *programming language* [p. 12.16]
7. *low-level* [p. 12.16]
8. *message* [p. 12.22]
9. *application generator* [p. 12.30]
10. *macro* [p. 12.31]

Complete the Table [p. 12.29]

ALGOL	ALGOrithmic Language, the first structured procedural language
APL	*A Programming Language, a scientific language designed to manipulate tables of numbers*
FORTH	Similar to C, used for device control applications
HYPERTALK	An object-oriented programming language developed by Apple to manipulate cards that can contain text, graphics, and sound
LISP	*LISt Processing, a language used for artificial intelligence applications*
LOGO	An educational tool used to teach programming and problem-solving to children
MODULA-2	*A successor to Pascal used for developing operating systems software*
PILOT	*Programmed Inquiry Learning Or Teaching, used to write computer-aided instruction programs*
PL/1	Programming Language One, a business and scientific language that combines many features of FORTRAN and COBOL
PROLOG	*PROgramming LOGic, used for development of expert systems*
SMALLTALK	*Object-oriented programming language*

Puzzle Answer

	P	R	O	G	R	A	M	M	I	N	G
B	A	S	I	C	E	C	R	U	O	**S**	N
L	O	G	L	**A**	D	C	O	B	O	L	I
R	P	G	⊞	**L**	O	O	P	I	N	G	K
E	T	E	S	A	**C**	B	**L**	O	G	I	C
L	I	T	N	U	O	**D**	J	⌨	⊖	**S**	E
B	X	**A**	P	L	D	T	S	**E**	**T**	Y	H
M	**E**	L	A	R	U	T	A	**N**	C	N	C
E	N	U	D	N	E	E	R	C	**S**	T	K
S	T	N	A	S	S	A	L	**C**	G	A	S
S	R	E	L	I	**P**	M	O	**C**	U	X	E
A	Y	**M**	G	N	I	G	G	U	**B**	E	**D**

CHAPTER 13
Security, Privacy, and Ethics

CHAPTER OVERVIEW

This chapter identifies the risks to computer security, the safeguards that can be taken to minimize these risks, and the issue of information privacy. Various computer security risks, including computer viruses, unauthorized access and use, hardware theft, software theft, and information theft, are detailed. You learn about safeguards that can be taken to address these risks, such as virus detection and removal, backup procedures, and a disaster recovery plan. Finally, computer ethics and information privacy are discussed.

CHAPTER OBJECTIVES

After completing this chapter, you will be able to:

- Identify the different types of security risks that can threaten computer systems
- Describe different ways computer systems can be safeguarded
- Describe how a computer virus works and the steps that can be taken to prevent viruses
- Explain why computer backup is important and how it is accomplished
- Discuss the steps in a disaster recovery plan
- Discuss issues relating to information privacy
- Discuss ethical issues with respect to the information age
- Specify security, privacy, and ethics issues that relate to the Internet

CHAPTER OUTLINE

I. Computer security: risks and safeguards [p. 13.2]

A computer security risk is _____

_____

A computer crime is _____

A. Computer viruses [p. 13.2]

(continued)

A computer virus is _____

_____

Four main types of viruses:

A boot sector virus _____

A file virus _____

A Trojan horse virus _____

A macro virus _____

Some viruses interrupt processing by temporarily freezing a computer system and displaying sounds or messages.

A logic bomb _____

A time bomb _____

A worm program _____

_____

B.   Virus detection and removal [p. 13.4]

Antivirus programs (vaccines) _____

_____

_____

A virus signature is _____

A polymorphic virus is _____

When a program file is inoculated, _____

_____

A stealth virus is _____

A rescue disk _____

_____

To protect against being infected by a computer virus:

•   _____

•   _____

•   _____

C.   Unauthorized access and use [p. 13.5]

Unauthorized access is _____

_____

Crackers are _____

The term hacker _____

Unauthorized use is _____

_____

The key to preventing both unauthorized access and unauthorized use of computers is _____

_____

Access controls are implemented by many commercial software packages through a process called identification (verifies the user is a valid user) and authentication (verifies the user is who he or she claims to be).

Three methods of authentication: remembered information, possessed objects, and biometric devices

1. Remembered information [p. 13.6]

    _____

    Techniques users can follow to create passwords:

    *   _____
    *   _____
    *   _____
    *   _____
    *   _____
    *   _____
    *   _____

    Sniffer programs _____

    With dialog authentication, _____

2. Possessed objects [p. 13.7]

    A possessed object is _____

    _____

    A personal identification number (PIN) _____

3. Biometric devices [p. 13.7]

    A biometric device is _____

    _____

    Types of biometric devices _____

    _____

    With a callback system, _____

    _____

    An organization should review _____

    Computer systems should record both successful and unsuccessful access attempts.

D. Hardware theft [p. 13.9]

    _____

    _____

    _____

E. Software theft [p. 13.10]

    _____

    Software piracy is _____

    The Business Systems Alliance (BSA) is _____

    A site license _____

F. Information theft [p. 13.11]

    _____

    _____

(continued)

Encryption is _____

_____

An encryption key is _____

A public key encryption uses _____

The data encryption standard (DES) is _____

The Clipper chip is _____

The government's key escrow plan _____

G. System failure [p. 13.13]

A system failure is _____

_____

Noise is _____

An undervoltage _____

A brownout is _____

A blackout is _____

An overvoltage, or power surge, occurs _____

A spike _____

A surge protector (surge suppressor) _____

_____

An uninterruptable power supply (UPS) is _____

_____

H. Backup procedures [p. 13.15]

A backup is _____

Backup procedures _____

Backup copies, which can be used to restore files (reload them on the computer) normally are kept

_____

A full backup _____

A differential backup _____

An incremental backup _____

In a three-generation backup policy, the grandfather is _____,

the father is _____, and the son is _____.

I. Disaster recovery plan [p. 13.17]

A disaster recovery plan is _____

_____

Four major components of a disaster recovery plan: _____,

_____, _____, and _____

1. The emergency plan [p. 13.17]

Specifies _____

Information contained in:

(1) _____

(2) _____

(3) _____

(4) _____

2. The backup plan [p. 13.18]

Specifies _____

Identifies:

(1) _____

(2) _____

(3) _____

A hot site is _____

A cold site is _____

Reciprocal backup relationships _____

_____

3. The recovery plan [p. 13.18]

Specifies _____

4. The test plan [p. 13.18]

Contains _____

_____

J. Developing a computer security plan [p. 13.19]

A computer security plan _____

_____

The plan should:

• _____

• _____

• _____

The goal of a computer security plan is _____

_____

II. Information privacy [p. 13.20]

Refers to _____

_____

Issues: _____

A. Unauthorized collection and use of information [p. 13.20]

_____

_____

Common points in laws regarding storage and disclosure of personal data:

(1) _____

_____

(continued)

(2) _____

_____

(3) _____

_____

(4) _____

_____

Several federal laws deal specifically with computers.

The 1986 Electronic Communications Privacy Act (ECPA) _____

_____

The 1988 Computer Matching and Privacy Protection Act _____

_____

The 1984 and 1994 Computer Fraud and Abuse Acts _____

_____

Fair Credit Report Act limits _____

B. Employee monitoring [p. 13.22]

_____

_____

III. Ethics and the information age [p. 13.23]

Computer ethics are _____

_____

Five areas of computer ethics: _____, _____,

_____, _____, and _____

A. Information accuracy [p. 13.23]

_____

_____

_____

B. Codes of conduct [p. 13.24]

Codes of conduct are _____

_____

IV. Internet security, privacy, and ethics issues [p. 13.25]

The widespread use of the Internet has _____

A. Internet security and privacy [p. 13.25]

_____

_____

A Secure Socket Layer (SSL) is _____

Certificates (digital IDs or digital signatures) are _____

_____

A cookie is _____

Cookies can be used _____

B. Objectionable materials on the Internet [p. 13.27]

_____

_____

The Communications Decency Act _____

_____

A rating system _____

V. Summary of security, privacy, and ethics [p. 13.28]

_____

_____

_____

TERMS

access controls [p. 13.5]
Active Badge system
     [p. 13.30]
antivirus programs [p. 13.4]
authentication [p. 13.5]

backup [p. 13.15]
backup plan [p. 13.18]
backup procedures [p. 13.15]
biometric device [p. 13.7]
blackout [p. 13.13]
boot sector virus [p. 13.3]
brownout [p. 13.13]
Business Software Alliance (BSA)
     [p. 13.10]

callback system [p. 13.8]
certificates [p. 13.26]
ciphertext [p. 13.11]
Clipper chip [p. 13.12]
codes of conduct [p. 13.24]
cold site [p. 13.18]
Communications Decency Act
     [p. 13.27]
computer crime [p. 13.2]
computer ethics [p. 13.23]
computer security plan
     [p. 13.19]
computer security risk
     [p. 13.2]
computer virus [p. 13.2]
computerized facial recognition
     (CFR) [p. 13.31]
cookie [p. 13.26]
crackers [p. 13.5]

data encryption standard
     (DES) [p 13.12]

dialog authentication [p. 13.7]
differential backup [p. 13.15]
digital IDs [p. 13.26]
digital signatures [p. 13.26]
dirty data [p. 13.23]
disaster recovery test plan
     [p. 13.18]

emergency plan [p. 13.17]
employee monitoring
     [p. 13.22]
encryption [p. 13.11, 13.26]
encryption key [p. 13.11]

father [p. 13.16]
file virus [p. 13.3]
full backup [p. 13.15]

grandfather [p. 13.16]

hacker [p. 13.5]
hot site [p. 13.18]

identification [p. 13.5]
incremental backup [p. 13.15]
information privacy [p. 13.20]
inoculated [p. 13.4]

key escrow [p. 13.12]

logic bomb [p. 13.3]

macro virus [p. 13.3]

noise [p. 13.13]

offsite [p. 13.15]
overvoltage [p. 13.13]

personal identification number
     (PIN) [p. 13.7]
plaintext [p. 13.11]
polymorphic virus [p. 13.4]

possessed object [p. 13.7]
power surge [p. 13.13]
public key encryption [p. 13.11]

reciprocal backup relationship
     [p. 13.18]
recovery plan [p. 13.17, 13.18]
remembered information
     authentication [p. 13.6]
rescue disk [p. 13.5]
restore [p. 13.15]

Secure Socket Layer (SSL)
     [p. 13.26]
site license [p. 13.11]
sniffer [p. 13.7]
software piracy [p. 13.10]
son [p. 13.16]
spike [p. 13.13]
stealth virus [p. 13.4]
surge protector [p. 13.14]
surge suppressor [p. 13.14]
system failure [p. 13.13]

three-generation backup policy
     [p. 13.16]
time bomb [p. 13.3]
Trojan horse virus [p. 13.3]

unauthorized access [p. 13.5]
unauthorized use [p. 13.5]
undervoltage [p. 13.13]
uninterruptable power supply
     (UPS) [p. 13.14]

vaccines [p. 13.4]
virus signature [p. 13.4]

worm [p. 13.3]

SELF TEST

True/False

_____ 1. Because a polymorphic virus is designed to use the same program code each time it attaches itself to another program or file, it is detected easily with a virus signature.

_____ 2. A virus that uses methods to avoid detection is called a Trojan horse.

_____ 3. The term hacker, although originally a positive term, also has become associated with people who try to break into computer systems.

_____ 4. A biometric device is any item that a user must carry to gain access to a computer facility, such as badges, cards, or keys.

_____ 5. Many organizations have written policies prohibiting the copying and use of copyrighted software.

_____ 6. Some organizations use available software packages, but most develop their own encryption methods.

_____ 7. Overvoltages can cause a loss of data but generally do not damage computer equipment.

_____ 8. Information privacy refers to the rights of individuals and organizations to deny or restrict the collection or use of information about them.

_____ 9. Employee monitoring involves the use of computers to observe, record, and review employee communications and keyboard activity.

_____ 10. Digital retouching is an area where legal precedents have long been established.

Matching

1. _____ computer security risk
2. _____ computer virus
3. _____ vaccine
4. _____ unauthorized access
5. _____ unauthorized use
6. _____ system failure
7. _____ backup procedure
8. _____ disaster recovery plan
9. _____ computer security plan
10. _____ codes of conduct

a. computer program designed to attach itself to and infect software or files with which it comes in contact

b. prolonged malfunction of a computer system caused by natural disasters or electrical power problems

c. describes the steps an organization would take to restore computer operations after a catastrophe

d. uninfected copy of certain operating system commands and essential computer information

e. any event that could cause a loss to equipment, software, data and information, or processing capability

f. also called an antivirus program, developed to protect against computer viruses

g. written guidelines that help determine whether a specific computer action is ethical or unethical

h. item a user must carry to gain access to a computer facility

i. gives an organization the right to install software on multiple computers at a single site

j. computer trespassing or using a computer system without permission

k. concerns rights of individuals and organizations to restrict the collection and use of information

l. involves the use of computers to observe, record, and review employee communications and activity

m. employing a computer system or computer data for unapproved or possibly illegal activities

n. summarizes the safeguards that are in place to protect an organization's information assets

o. specifies a regular plan of copying and storing key data and program files

Multiple Choice

_____ 1. What is a boot sector virus?

    a. a virus that replaces the program used to start a system with a modified, infected version of the program

    b. a virus that inserts virus code into program files and then spreads to any program that accesses the infected file

    c. a virus that hides within or is designed to look like a legitimate program

    d. a virus designed to modify its program code each time it attaches itself to another program or file

_____ 2. What type of program contained in a virus performs an activity when a certain action has occurred, such as an employee being terminated?

    a. a time bomb

    b. a logic bomb

    c. a bug bomb

    d. a worm

_____ 3. What is remembered information authentication?

    a. a form of biometric device that usually identifies the application that will be used, such as accounting, sales, or manufacturing

    b. a form of access control usually assigned by the organization that identifies hackers

    c. a form of access control in which an item of personal information is chosen from a file and asked of the user

    d. consists of a confidential word or series of characters known only by the user and matching an entry in a security file

_____ 4. For most desktop and larger computer systems, which of the following usually can be prevented by physical access controls such as locked doors and windows?

    a. unauthorized access

    b. information theft

    c. unauthorized use

    d. hardware theft

_____ 5. What does a site license allow an organization to do?

    a. install software on multiple computers at a single site

    b. install software that resides on a server computer and can be shared among network users

    c. install software that users may try out on their own before paying a fee

    d. install software that is not copyrighted and can therefore be distributed among users

_____ 6. A surge protector is used to protect against which of the following?

    a. brownouts

    b. overvoltages

    c. blackouts

    d. noise

(continued)

_____ 7. What is an advantage of a full backup?
   a.   fastest recovery method
   b.   shortest backup time
   c.   requires minimal space to backup
   d.   only most recent changes are saved

_____ 8. What component of a disaster recovery plan contains information for simulating different levels of disasters and recording an organization's ability to recover?
   a.   the emergency plan
   b.   the backup plan
   c.   the recovery plan
   d.   the test plan

_____ 9. What law prohibits unauthorized access to federal government computers and the transmission of harmful computer code such as viruses?
   a.   1988 Computer Matching and Privacy Act
   b.   1986 Electronic Communications Privacy Act
   c.   1984 and 1994 Computer Fraud and Abuse Acts
   d.   1974 Privacy Act

_____ 10. Which of the following is *not* an area of computer ethics?
   a.   information accuracy
   b.   computer system failure
   c.   codes of ethical conduct
   d.   information privacy

Fill in the Blanks

1. Unlike a virus, a(n) _____ program does not attach itself to another program but is designed to repeatedly copy itself in memory or on a disk drive until no memory or disk space remains.

2. When a program file is _____, information about the file is stored in a separate file that a vaccine program can use to tell if a virus has tampered with the program file.

3. Many commercial software packages are designed to implement _____ through a process called identification and authentication.

4. Unauthorized _____ programs can copy passwords as they are entered.

5. A(n) _____ is one that verifies personal characteristics such as fingerprints, voice patterns, signature, hand size, and retinal patterns to identify a user.

6. A formula that uses a code, called a(n) _____, is used to convert plaintext into ciphertext.

7. A momentary overvoltage, called a(n) _____, occurs when the power increase lasts for less than one millisecond (one thousandth of a second).

8. _____ storage normally is used for backup copies so a single disaster will not destroy both the primary and the backup copy of data.

9. In a three-generation backup policy, the most recent copy of the file is called the _____.

10. A(n) _____, one of the four major components of a disaster recovery plan, specifies the steps to be taken immediately after a disaster strikes.

Complete the Table

DATE	LAW	PURPOSE
1996	_____ _____	Penalties for theft of information across state lines, threats against networks, and computer system trespassing.
1994	**Computer Abuse Amendments Act**	_____ _____
1992	_____	Extends privacy of Cable Communications Policy Act of 1984 to include cellular and other wireless services.
1988	**Computer Matching and Privacy Protection Act**	_____ _____ _____
1986	_____ _____	Provides the same right of privacy protection for the postal delivery service and telephone companies to the new forms of electronic communications, such as voice mail, e-mail, and cellular telephones.
1984	**Computer Fraud and Abuse Act**	_____ _____
1978	_____	Strictly outlines procedures federal agencies must follow when looking at customer records in banks.
1974	_____	Forbids federal agencies from allowing information to be used for a reason other than which it was collected.
1974	**Family Educational Rights and Privacy Act**	_____ _____ _____
1970	**Fair Credit Reporting Act**	_____ _____ _____ _____

Things to Think About

1. Three methods of authentication are remembered information, possessed objects, and biometric devices. What are the advantages of each method? What are the disadvantages?

2. Why has software theft, or software piracy, become a major problem with the increased use of personal computers?

3. When providing for an alternate computer facility, what type of organization would be most likely to use a hot site? What type of organization would be most likely to use a cold site? What type of organization might choose instead to enter into a reciprocal backup relationship with another firm?

4. The goal of a computer security plan is to match an appropriate level of safeguards against the identified risks. What is meant by this?

Puzzle

The terms described by each phrase below and on the next page are written in code. Break the code by writing the correct term above the coded word. Then, use your broken code to decrypt the final sentence.

Trojan horse

1. type of virus that hides within or looks like a legitimate program

2. a specific pattern of virus code

3. used to restart a computer correctly after a virus is detected

4. people who deliberately try to illegally access computer systems

5. access control process that verifies the user's identity

6. code that identifies the user, usually assigned by the organization

7. form of authentication in which personal information is asked of the user

8. type of system sometimes used to authenticate remote users

9. distribution of software to persons who have not legally purchased it

10. gives the right to install software on multiple computers

11. process of converting readable data into unreadable characters

12. the unreadable characters produced by encryption process

13. the code used in an encryption formula

14. prolonged drop in electrical power

15. occurs when incoming electrical power is significantly above normal

16. any unwanted signal mixed with normal voltage entering a computer

17. a copy of information stored on a computer

18. type of backup that copies only files altered since the last full backup

19. in a three-generation backup policy, the oldest copy of a file

20. empty facility that can accommodate necessary computer resources

SELF TEST ANSWERS

True/False

1. *F* [p. 13.4]
2. *F* [p. 13.4]
3. *T* [p. 13.5]
4. *F* [p. 13.7]
5. *T* [p. 13.10]
6. *F* [p. 13.12]
7. *F* [p. 13.13]
8. *T* [p. 13.20]
9. *T* [p. 13.22]
10. *F* [p. 13.24]

Matching

1. *e* [p. 13.2]
2. *a* [p. 13.2]
3. *f* [p. 13.4]
4. *j* [p. 13.5]
5. *m* [p. 13.5]
6. *b* [p. 13.13]
7. *o* [p. 13.15]
8. *c* [p. 13.17]
9. *n* [p. 13.19]
10. *g* [p. 13.24]

Multiple Choice

1. *a* [p. 13.3]
2. *b* [p. 13.3]
3. *d* [p. 13.6]
4. *d* [p. 13.9]
5. *a* [p. 13.11]
6. *b* [p. 13.14]
7. *a* [p. 13.15]
8. *d* [p. 13.18]
9. *c* [p. 13.22]
10. *b* [p. 13.23]

Fill in the Blanks

1. *worm* [p. 13.3]
2. *inoculated* [p. 13.4]
3. *access controls* [p. 13.5]
4. *sniffer* [p. 13.7]
5. *biometric device* [p. 13.7]
6. *encryption key* [p. 13.11]
7. *spike* [p. 13.13]
8. *Offsite* [p. 13.15]
9. *son* [p. 13.16]
10. *emergency plan* [p. 13.17]

Complete the Table [p. 13.21]

DATE	LAW	PURPOSE
1996	*National Information Infrastructure Protection Act*	Penalties for theft of information across state lines, threats against networks, and computer system trespassing.
1994	**Computer Abuse Amendments Act**	*Amends 1984 act to outlaw transmission of harmful computer code such as viruses.*
1992	*Cable Act*	Extends privacy of Cable Communications Policy Act of 1984 to include cellular and other wireless services.
1988	**Computer Matching and Privacy Protection Act**	*Regulates the use of government data to determine the eligibility of individuals for federal benefits.*
1986	*Electronic Communications Privacy Act (ECPA)*	Provides the same right of privacy protection for the postal delivery service and telephone companies to new forms of electronic communications, such as voice mail, e-mail, and cellular telephones.
1984	**Computer Fraud and Abuse Act**	*Outlaws unauthorized access of federal government computers.*
1978	*Right to Financial Privacy Act*	Strictly outlines procedures federal agencies must follow when looking at customer records in banks.
1974	*Privacy Act*	Forbids federal agencies from allowing information to be used for a reason other than which it was collected.
1974	**Family Educational Rights and Privacy Act**	*Gives students and parents access to school records and limits disclosure of records to unauthorized parties.*
1970	**Fair Credit Reporting Act**	*Prohibits credit reporting agencies from releasing credit information to unauthorized people and allows consumers to review their credit records.*

Puzzle Answer

1. type of virus that hides within or looks like a legitimate program

2. a specific pattern of virus code

3. used to restart a computer correctly after a virus is detected

4. people who deliberately try to illegally access computer systems

5. access control process that verifies the user's identity

6. code that identifies the user, usually assigned by the organization

7. form of authentication in which personal information is asked of the user

8. type of system sometimes used to authenticate remote users

9. distribution of software to persons who have not legally purchased it

10. gives the right to install software on multiple computers

11. process of converting readable data into unreadable characters

12. the unreadable characters produced by the encryption process

13. the code used in an encryption formula

14. prolonged drop in electrical power

15. occurs when incoming electrical power is significantly above normal

16. any unwanted signal mixed with normal voltage entering a computer

17. a copy of information stored on a computer

Trojan horse

virus signature

rescue disk

crackers

authentication

user ID

dialog

callback

software piracy

site license

encryption

ciphertext

encryption key

brownout

overvoltage

noise

backup

18. type of backup that copies only files altered since the last full backup

differential

⟨glyphs⟩

19. in a three generation backup policy, the oldest copy of a file

grandfather

⟨glyphs⟩

cold site

20. empty facility that can accommodate necessary computer resources

⟨glyphs⟩

One method of committing computer crime is to

⟨glyphs⟩

modify input before it is processed, a procedure

⟨glyphs⟩

known as "data diddling."

⟨glyphs⟩

C H A P T E R   14
Multimedia

CHAPTER OVERVIEW

This chapter introduces you to multimedia and examines in detail each of the individual components: text, graphics, animation, audio, and video. Next, you learn about the variety of multimedia applications and how each of these applications is used in industry, home, education, health, and entertainment. The equipment needed to make multimedia applications and presentations is described. You learn that building a multimedia application is similar to developing any system and follows a standard process with several phases. Finally, three popular authoring software packages are presented along with a discussion of the approach each takes to building a multimedia presentation.

CHAPTER OBJECTIVES

After completing this chapter, you will be able to:

- Define multimedia
- Describe types of media used in multimedia applications
- List and describe the different uses of multimedia applications
- List and describe the different types of multimedia equipment
- Explain how a multimedia application is developed
- Describe several multimedia authoring software packages

CHAPTER OUTLINE

I. What is multimedia? [p. 14.2]

Multimedia refers to _____

_____

Interactive multimedia _____

_____

A. Text [p. 14.2]

Text is _____

_____

(continued)

Multimedia applications also use text-based menus _____

B. Interactive links [p. 14.3]

Hyperlinks or interactive links are _____

Hotwords are _____

Hyperlinks allow _____

C. Still graphic images [p. 14.4]

Still graphic images are _____

Graphic typically refers to _____

Graphics used in multimedia applications are obtained in several ways.

Graphics play an important role _____

_____

D. Animation [p. 14.5]

Refers to _____

Animation can be used _____

_____

E. Audio [p. 14.5]

Is sound _____

Audio provides _____

F. Video [p. 14.6]

Is comprised of _____

_____

To use video in multimedia applications, _____

_____

Video compression works by _____

_____

The Moving Pictures Experts Group (MPEG) has _____

_____

II. Multimedia applications [p. 14.7]

Used by _____

Simulations are _____

A. Computer-based training [p. 14.7]

Computer-based training (CBT) is _____

CBT allows _____

Interactive training software _____

_____

Computer-based training provides _____

_____

Besides testing and self-diagnostic features that allow verification that information has been learned, CBT offers many other advantages over traditional training methods:

- _____ — _____
- Reduced training time — _____
- _____ — _____
- Reduced training costs — _____
- _____ — _____

Multimedia applications also appeal to _____

B. Special education [p. 14.8]

Multimedia applications are used for _____

Major benefits to the learning disabled include _____

_____

C. Electronic books and references [p. 14.9]

Electronic books are _____

These texts contain _____

Electronic reference texts are _____

_____

Two areas where multimedia reference texts are playing an important role are _____

D. How-to guides [p. 14.10]

How-to guides _____

E. Magazines [p. 14.11]

Multimedia magazines often _____

They include _____

Multimedia magazines usually are distributed using CD-ROMs or the World Wide Web.

F. Entertainment [p. 14.12]

_____

_____

G. Virtual reality [p. 14.12]

Virtual reality (VR) is _____

_____

More advanced forms of VR require _____

_____

Web-based VR applications _____

Uses of VR include _____

_____

H. Information kiosks [p. 14.14]

An information kiosk is _____

_____

(continued)

Kiosks typically are _____

_____

Kiosks provide _____

_____

Kiosks are used in marketing by _____

_____

I.   Electronic marketing and sales [p. 14.15]

_____

_____

J.   The Internet and the World Wide Web applications [p. 14.15]

The Web uses many types of media to deliver information and enhance the Web experience.

Graphics and animations are _____

_____

Some authoring software packages allow _____

_____

III. Multimedia equipment [p. 14.16]

Equipment selection is an important process in both the development and delivery of multimedia products.

A.   Multimedia personal computer [p. 14.16]

Is a computer system that _____

_____

The MPC level or specification is _____

_____

MPC level 2 will allow _____

_____

MPC level 3 will allow _____

_____

MMX™ technology is _____

_____

Multimedia extensions are _____

Besides the required components, _____

_____

1.   Sound card [p. 14.17]

Is a circuit board that houses processors used to provide both audio input and output

The typical sound card has _____

The audio digitizer is _____

The wavetable synthesizer has _____

The mixer combines _____

2.   CD-ROM drive [p. 14.18]

The storage capacity of a CD-ROM _____

_____

The faster the transfer rate _____

_____

Most CD-ROMs are internal, have headphone plugs, and _____

_____

3. Speakers [p. 14.18]

_____

_____

4. Video display [p. 14.18]

   To effectively display multimedia _____

   _____

   _____

B. Overhead projection systems [p. 14.19]

   To connect an MPC to a large-screen TV you need _____

   _____

   For presenting to even larger groups, an _____

   An LCD projector panel is _____

   A video projector is _____

   _____

C. Video capture card [p. 14.20]

   Is an expansion card _____

   _____

   Digital video interleave (DVI) _____

   _____

   DVI is capable of _____

   _____

D. Scanners, digital cameras, and photo CDs [p. 14.20]

   A color scanner is _____

   The basic software that comes with a scanner _____

   A digital camera _____

   Photo CD system _____

E. Laser disks [p. 14.22]

   Are part of a read-only video disk system based _____

   Constant angular velocity (CAV) refers _____

   _____

   Constant linear velocity (CLV) _____

   _____

(continued)

MCI (media control interface) commands _____

_____

F.   Video overlay cards [p. 14.22]

A video overlay card is used _____

_____

Disadvantages of such systems are _____

_____

IV. Developing multimedia applications [p. 14.23]

As with all program development, developing multimedia applications follows a standard process with several phases.

A.   Analysis [p. 14.23]

During the analysis phase, _____

_____

_____

B.   Design [p. 14.24]

During the design phase, _____

_____

A tool called the project script _____

_____

Screen design should consider _____

_____

_____

C.   Production [p. 14.25]

Multimedia production is _____

_____

During authoring, _____

_____

D.   Multimedia authoring software [p. 14.25]

Multimedia Authoring software allows _____

_____

_____

Important factors to consider when selecting a multimedia authoring software package:

-   _____

-   _____

-   Responsiveness of vendor's service and technical support

-   _____

-   _____

-   _____

-   _____

The major difference among authoring software packages is the ease of use for development.

1. ToolBook [p. 14.26]

   ToolBook, from Asymetrix Corporation, uses _____

   _____

   The program or application you build is called _____

   OpenScript is _____

   Widgets are _____

   A number of Widgets are provided by ToolBook in _____

   Widgets eliminate much _____

   ToolBook can be used to convert _____

   By using the Internet students and employees at remote locations can participate in distributed learning or distance learning courses.

2. Authorware [p. 14.28]

   Authorware Professional uses a _____

   A fixed set of icons, called a _____, are dragged to a flow line _____

   _____

   The graphic toolbox contains _____

   _____

   Shockwave is _____

3. Director [p. 14.30]

   Uses the metaphor of a theater or movie production to produce highly interactive multimedia applications.

   The Cast window serves _____

   The Score window allows _____

   The Paint window contains _____

   Lingo is _____

   As with Authorware, Director applications can be viewed on the Web with the Shockwave browser plug-in.

V. Summary of multimedia [p. 14.31]

_____

_____

TERMS

analysis [p. 14.23]
animation [p. 14.5]
audio [p. 14. 5]
authoring [p. 14.25]
Authorware [p. 14.28]

book [p. 14.26]

Cast window [p. 14.30]
CAV (constant angular velocity)
   [p. 14.22]
CD-ROM [p. 14.18]

CLV (constant linear velocity)
   [p. 14.22]
color scanner [p. 14.20]
computer-based training (CBT)
   [p. 14.7]
courseware [p. 14.7]

design [p. 14.24]
developing multimedia
   applications [p. 14.23]
digital camera [p. 14.21]

digital video interleave (DVI)
   [p. 14.20]
Director [p. 14.30]
distance learning [p. 14.28]
distributed learning [p. 14.28]

edutainment [p. 14.12]
electronic books [p. 14.9]
electronic reference [p. 14.9]

flow line [p. 14.28]

(continued)

graphic [p. 14.4]

hotwords [p. 14.3, 14.9]
how-to guides [p. 14.10]
hybrid CD-ROM [p. 14.33]

information kiosk [p. 14.14]
interactive links [p. 14.3]
interactive multimedia [p. 14.2]

LCD projector panel [p. 14.19]
Lingo [p. 14.30]

MCI (media control interface)
  commands [p. 14.22]
MMX™ technology [p. 14.16]
MPC level [p. 14.16]
MPEG (Moving Pictures Experts
  Group) [p. 14.6]
multimedia [p. 14.2]
multimedia applications [p. 14.7]

multimedia authoring software
  [p. 14.25]
multimedia extensions [p. 14.16]
multimedia magazines [p. 14.11]
multimedia personal computer
  [p. 14.16]

NautilusCD [p. 14.11]
NTSC (National Television
  System Committee) [p. 14.19]
NTSC converter [p. 14.19]

OpenScript [p. 14.26]
overhead projection system
  [p. 14.19]

page [p. 14.26]
Paint window [p. 14.30]
Photo CD system [p. 14.21]
production [p. 14.25]
project script [p. 14.24]

Score window [p. 14.30]

Shockwave [p. 14.29]
simulations [p. 14.7]
sound card [p. 14.17]
speakers [p. 14.18]
specification [p. 14.16]
still graphic images [p. 14.4]

text [p. 14.2]
ToolBook [p. 14.26]
toolbox [p. 14.28]

video [p. 14.6]
video capture card [p. 14.20]
video compression [p. 14.6]
video display [p. 14.18]
video overlay card [p. 14.22]
video projector [p. 14.19]
virtual reality (VR) [p. 14.12]

Widget Catalog [p. 14.27]
widgets [p. 14.27]

SELF TEST

True/False

1. Text is the fundamental component in many multimedia programs.

2. The purpose of hyperlinks in multimedia applications is to allow quick access to information in a nonlinear fashion.

3. Text plays the most important role in multimedia applications because people are used to reading so much.

4. Video compression works by taking advantage of the fact that only a small portion of the image changes from frame to frame.

5. Multimedia presentations only appeal to image and visually oriented learning styles.

6. Virtual reality applications allow the user to experience an artificial environment through interactively exploring and manipulating the environment.

7. Multimedia personal computer specifications (MPC) are strictly established by Microsoft and Intel to work with the Pentium processor MMX™ technology.

8. Most people do not realize it, but they easily and quickly can hook their computers directly to their large-screen TV sets for displays of multimedia animation.

9. A color scanner converts images into analog format for use in multimedia applications.

10. To show video from a laser disk player, a separate monitor or projector is needed because the computer monitor is used to display the media control interface commands.

Matching

1.	_____	graphic	a. computer based models of real-life situations that are used in training
2.	_____	MPEG	b. use of computer-aided instruction to teach specific skills
3.	_____	computer-based training	c. allows you to display single frames of video sequence or play a clip frame by frame
4.	_____	hotwords	d. uses a data entry device to transcribe data from source documents into a computer
5.	_____	multimedia magazine	e. special application software used to write multimedia presentations
6.	_____	information kiosks	f. allows both the MCI commands and the video from a laser disk to appear on the computer monitor
7.	_____	Photo CD system	g. serve as hyperlinks to display a definition, play a sound, or show a graphic
8.	_____	constant angular velocity	h. refers to still images; contains no movement
9.	_____	constant linear velocity	i. a computer-based presentation that incorporates more than one media
10.	_____	video overlay card	j. computerized information or reference center that allows the selection of various options

k. a write-once compact disk that stores photographic images

l. can store more information than a CAV disk, but is not suitable for showing single frames

m. similar in appearance to print-based counter part and includes audio and video clips

n. a special CD-ROM disk that can hold 120 minutes of full-motion video

o. developed standards for video compression and decompression

Multiple Choice

_____ 1. What is multimedia?
   a. any presentation that contains hyperlinks
   b. the use of some form of animation graphics in a presentation
   c. any computer-based presentation software that integrates at least two or more elements of text, color, graphics, animation, audio, and video
   d. interactive video computer-based training

_____ 2. Why do graphics play an important role in multimedia presentations?
   a. because clip art is free, reducing costs of presentations
   b. because Photo CDs add more color and variations to applications
   c. because people are more visually oriented than ever
   d. because most multimedia is presented on the Web

_____ 3. Why does animation convey information more vividly than just text and graphics?
   a. animation provides a better understanding of a process than does a written explanation
   b. animation is more entertaining than still graphics
   c. animation is proven to hold attention spans 10 times longer than text and graphics presentations
   d. more information can be conveyed in a short animation presentation than an entire text

(continued)

_____ 4. Which of the following is *not* an advantage of CBT over traditional training?
   a.   students can progress at their own pace
   b.   large numbers of students can use the course simultaneously
   c.   trainers can spend more time with trainees
   d.   the same information can be conveyed in different ways

_____ 5. How does a simulation offer students a unique instructional experience?
   a.   students can learn in hazardous, emergency, or real-world situations without risk
   b.   grading of simulations always is easier
   c.   the use of simulations is directed toward a certain type of learning style
   d.   simulations are easy to program and easily modified

_____ 6. Which of the following is used by electronic books to enhance the explanation of a topic or provide additional information?
   a.   graphics
   b.   sound
   c.   video
   d.   all of the above

_____ 7. In which of the following ways are multimedia magazines different from regular print magazines?
   a.   use of additional media to convey information
   b.   have large selection of articles
   c.   include departments or editorials
   d.   all of the above

_____ 8. What is an information kiosk?
   a.   a large screen display used at sporting events, that displays other information during breaks
   b.   customer centered computerized order desks used at specialty and discount stores
   c.   computer-based training terminals designed for the physically disabled
   d.   a computerized information center that allows selection of various options to find specific information

_____ 9. What is the most important factor to consider when purchasing a CD-ROM drive for a multimedia system?
   a.   storage capacity
   b.   speed
   c.   whether it uses optical or magnetic storage techniques
   d.   all of the above

_____ 10. What is the difference between a digital camera and a regular camera?
   a.   a digital camera uses small reusable disks to store the images
   b.   a digital camera also can record animation
   c.   only pictures taken with a digital camera can be transferred to a Photo CD
   d.   digital pictures are transferred to the computer with a scanner

Fill in the Blanks

1.   _____ is a multimedia application that accepts input from the user by means of the keyboard or pointing device and performs some action in response.

2.   Graphics play an important role in multimedia because people are more _____ oriented than ever.

3.   _____ refers to moving graphic images.

4.   As with animation, integrating _____ into a multimedia application allows you to provide information not possible through any other method of communication in a computer environment.

5. Video is comprised of photographic images that display at speeds of _____ frames per second and provide the appearance of motion in real-time.

6. Interactive training software called _____ also can be distributed on CD-ROM or shared over a network.

7. _____ are products that allow you to plan, learn practical new skills, and have fun in the process.

8. A(n) _____ is a circuit board that houses processors used to provide both audio input and output.

9. _____ is the organization that sets the standards for most video and broadcast television equipment.

10. _____ allows you to combine text, graphics, animation, audio, and video into a finished application.

Complete the Table

	MPC Level 2 Specifications	MPC Level 3 Specifications
Date introduced	May 1993	_____
CPU	_____	75 MHz Pentium
_____	At least 4 megabytes of RAM (8 megabytes recommended)	_____ 8 megabytes of RAM
_____ Magnetic storage	_____ _____	Floppy disk drive, hard drive (540 MB minimum)
_____	Double-speed (2x)	_____
Audio	_____	16-bit wavetable, MIDI playback
_____ Video display	At least 640 x 480 with 65,536 (64K) colors	_____ _____
_____ Input	_____ _____	101-key keyboard (or functional equivalent), two-button mouse
_____	Serial port, parallel port, MIDI I/O port, joystick port	Serial port, parallel port, MIDI I/O port, joystick port
System software	Compatibility with Windows 3.1/Windows 3.0 plus multimedia extensions	_____

Things to Think About

1. In what circumstances can multimedia computer-based training (CBT) be better than a having a teacher? In what circumstances is a teacher better than computer-based training?

2. Will electronic books ever replace hard copy printed texts that we use now? What about reference books? What about other types of books, like novels, cookbooks, and so on?

3. Of all the uses for authoring software listed in Figure 14-38 on page 14.31, which do you think will become outdated as technology changes? What other types of uses not listed do you foresee as possible developments for the future?

4. What are your learning styles? What methods do you think you learn from best or most effectively? How can multimedia improve your ability to learn more?

Puzzle

Write the word described by each clue in the puzzle below. The first letter of each word already appears in the puzzle. Words may be written forward or downward only.

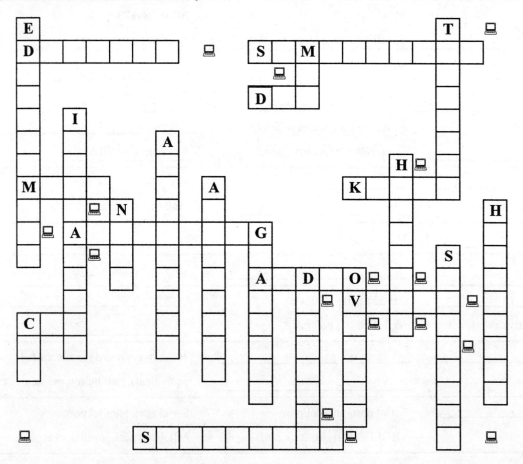

a type of multimedia application that accepts input from the user by some means and performs an action in response

allows user to access information quickly in a nonlinear fashion

typically refers to images that contain no movement

refers to moving graphic images

sound that has been digitized and stored in some form for replay

comprised of photographic images displayed at high speeds to provide appearance of motion

click on these to display a definition, play a sound, show a graphic

an experience meant to entertain and educate

computerized information or reference center

the circuit board that houses processors used to provide audio input and output

abbreviation for the organization that sets the standards for most broadcast equipment

compression capable of reducing size of file while maintaining image quality

type of camera that works like a regular camera, but uses a small reusable disk to store images

abbreviation for this type of format that allows you to display a single frame of video sequence or play a clip frame by frame

abbreviation for type of format that is not as well suited for showing single frames

abbreviation for type of commands used to send instructions from the computer to laser disk player

type of video card that allows a computer monitor to display both MCI commands and video from a laser disk

type of multimedia software that allows combination of text, graphics, animation, audio, and video

the authoring software that builds application software using the metaphor of a book

the authoring software that builds application software using the metaphor of a flowchart

the authoring software that builds application software using the metaphor of a theater or movie production

Web browser plug-in needed to run Authorware or ToolBook applications

SELF TEST ANSWERS

True/False
1. T [p. 14.2]
2. T [p. 14.3]
3. F [p. 14.4]
4. T [p. 14.6]
5. F [p. 14.8]
6. T [p. 14.12]
7. F [p. 14.16]
8. F [p. 14.19]
9. F [p. 14.20]
10. T [p. 14.22]

Matching
1. h [p. 14.4]
2. o [p. 14.6]
3. b [p. 14.7]
4. g [p. 14.9]
5. m [p. 14.11]
6. j [p. 14.14]
7. k [p. 14.21]
8. c [p. 14.22]
9. l [p. 14.22]
10. f [p. 14.22]

Multiple Choice
1. c [p. 14.2]
2. c [p. 14.4]
3. a [p. 14.5]
4. b [p. 14.8]
5. a [p. 14.8]
6. d [p. 14.9]
7. a [p. 14.11]
8. d [p. 14.14]
9. b [p. 14.18]
10. a [p. 14.21]

Fill in the Blanks
1. Interactive multimedia [p. 14.2]
2. visually [p. 14.4]
3. Animation [p. 14.5]
4. audio [p. 14.5]
5. 15 to 30 [p. 14.6]
6. courseware [p. 14.7]
7. How-to guides [p. 14.10]
8. sound card [p. 14.17]
9. NTSC (National Television System Committee) [p. 14.19]
10. Multimedia authoring software [p. 14.25]

Complete the Table [p. 14.17]

	MPC Level 2 Specifications	MPC Level 3 Specifications
Date introduced	May 1993	*June 1995*
CPU	*25 MHz 486SX*	75 MHz Pentium
RAM	At least 4 megabytes of RAM (8 megabytes recommended)	8 megabytes of RAM
Magnetic storage	*Floppy disk drive, hard drive* *(160 MB minimum)*	Floppy disk drive, hard drive (540 MB minimum)
Optical storage	Double-speed (2x)	*Quad-speed (4X)*
Audio	*16-bit*	16-bit wavetable, MIDI playback
Video display	At least 640 x 480 with 65,536 (64K) colors	*At least 640 x 480, with 65,536* *(64K) colors; MPEG-1 (full-screen video)*
Input	*101-key keyboard (or functional* *equivalent), two-button mouse*	101-key keyboard (or functional equivalent), two-button mouse
I/O	Serial port, parallel port, MIDI I/O port, joystick port	Serial port, parallel port, MIDI I/O port, joystick port
System software	Compatibility with Windows 3.1/Windows 3.0 plus multimedia extensions	*Compatibility with Windows 3.1/* *Windows 3.0 plus multimedia* *extensions*

Puzzle Answer

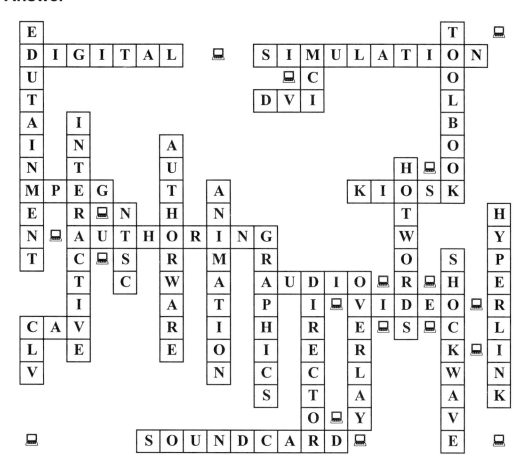